712
CSX

2625
2625

CSX

BRIAN SOLOMON

MBI

Dedication

To Connie Daniel, my favorite aunt.

First published in 2005 by MBI, an imprint of MBI Publishing Company, Galtier Plaza, Suite 200, 380 Jackson Street, St. Paul, MN 55101-3885 USA

ISBN 0-7603-1796-8

On the Front Cover: On February 20, 2004, CSX SD60M 8785 leads a freight between Petersburg and Jarratt, Virginia on the former Atlantic Coast Line mainline. *Brian Solomon*

Endpaper: A CSX route map. *Otto M. Vondrak*

On the frontispiece: CSX AC4400CW No. 50 leads 150 empty hoppers west on the former C&O James River Subdivision at Lick Run, Virginia, as the afternoon sun sets on Rich Patch Mountain on December 6, 2002. The James River Subdivision was built on the towpath of the James River and Kanawha canal between Clifton Forge and Richmond. The resulting favorable river level grade makes this route mandatory for eastbound loads and preferable for westbound empties. *T. S. Hoover*

On the title page: A brand new CSX SD70MAC leads a train of empty coal hoppers across the viaduct in Cumberland, Maryland, on September 27, 1997. Once this train is west of Keyser, West Virginia, it will tackle the famous Seventeen Mile Grade on the old B&O West End a line CSX call its Mountain Subdivision. The purchase of 25 GM SD70MACs in 1997 was CSX's first significant purchase of Electro-Motive Division locomotives in a dozen years. Except for 10 SD60s delivered in 1989 as compensation for the poorly performing SD50s, CSX had only ordered new GE locomotives. *Brian Solomon*

On the back cover 1: A road slug set consisting of a former GP30 leading and a GP40 operate a mine run hauling coal loads at North Edjouet, Kentucky, in May 1998. This run will terminate at North Hazard, Kentucky, one of several principle coal gathering yards on the former L&N. CSX operates a maze of coal lines throughout central Appalachia. *W. M. Beecher Jr.*

On the back cover 2: The sun sets on Conrail. In May 1999, just two days before Conrail operations were officially split between CSX and Norfolk Southern, an eastward multilevel train catches the glint of the setting sun as it rolls along the Mohawk River at Guy Park, west of Amsterdam, New York. Today this section of the former New York Central Water Level Route is a busy CSX freight corridor. *Brian Solomon*

Editorial: Amy Glaser
Design: Chris Fayers

Printed in China

Contents

Acknowledgments

While working on this book, many people not familiar with the intricacies of North American freight railroad operations would ask me, "What is CSX?" My simple response is CSX is the largest freight railroad in the eastern United States. Never mind its complex history or the wide scope of its contemporary operations. Ten years ago while traveling in western Maryland, I visited Altamont Tower at the top of the Seventeen Mile Grade. The operator and I were discussing railroad operations. Opening my mouth—often an error—I mentioned "CSX . . .," and the operator cut me off right there. "Son," he said, turning away from his control panel to look me in the eye, "the railroad is the B&O; CSX is what they print on the paychecks." There was still fierce loyalty to CSX's predecessors by its employees, shippers, and observers. Today, this has changed. In speaking with Doug Riddell—a career railroader who hired on with SCL in the 1970s and now runs from Amtrak—he tells me that so many of the old guard have retired and the ranks of railroaders are now filled with younger people who have only known CSX. Yet CSX is so big and covers so much territory, it leaves me to ask: What part of CSX matters most to you?

Trying to digest more than 175 years of CSX's history, operations, equipment, and technology has been a daunting task. While this book was in production for just a year, in reality I've spent most of my life around the railroads that comprise today's CSX. I've read just about everything I could find on its predecessors. I've spent thousands of hours exploring and photographing its system. I could not have done this without the help of many people. My father introduced me to railroads, and in my formative years he brought me to watch trains of the New York Central, Penn Central, and B&O among other lines. My brother Seán has accompanied me on numerous trips along the old B&O and Boston & Albany lines. My mother, Maureen, has encouraged and fostered my interest in photography, writing, and railways. I've often traveled with fellow photographers and each has lent his or her own perspective, assisting in the making of photographs; among them are: T. S. Hoover, Doug Eisele, Tim Doherty, Pat Yough, Michael L. Gardner, Otto M. Vondrak, George and Candy Pitarys, Don Marson, Brian Jennison, Doug Moore, Brandon Delany, Howard Ande, Norman Yellin, John Peters, Robert A. Buck, Will Holloway, M. Ross Valentine, Brian Plant, Pete Ruesch, Marshall Beecher, Mike Abalos, Charlie Streetman, and Mike Danneman. Special thanks to J. D. Schmid for inspiring my work with his own images of CSX. Many photographers have contributed their own images and images from their collections. Each is appropriately credited. I'm indebted to their generosity. Making railway photographs requires a degree of patience, skill, and a sense of adventure that goes well beyond ordinary activities.

Fortunately, I'm acquainted with many people who are more informed on matters relating to CSX and its history than I. Thanks to John P. Hankey for tours of the B&O in Maryland and for elucidating elements of B&O's history; to T. S. Hoover for the use of his library and his detailed explanations of B&O, C&O, and Clinchfield history and operations, a better understanding of modern motive power, and visits to Pennsylvania and Virginia; to Pat Yough for tours of the Hudson Line, expert map work, help with proofing, and for access to his library; to Tim Doherty for discussion of transport planning, operations, Conrail history, and for showing me milepost 44 on the River Line; to Jon Roma for better understanding of B&O electromechanical signal equipment and towers; to Ryan Krengel for explanations of Bee Line operations; and special thanks to Doug Riddell for tours of Richmond and vicinity and for detailed explanations of ACL, SAL, SCL, C&O, and RF&P operations and history. There are few who have Doug's talent for simultaneously informing and entertaining. Thanks to my father for the use of his ever growing railroad library and for proofreading. Thanks to the Irish Railway Record Society in Dublin for unrestricted use of their library, and thanks to Compleat Communications in Monson, Massachusetts, for office support. Thanks to Otto M. Vondrak for drawing maps. There is a wealth of literature relating to CSX and its components. Richard Saunders' books on railroad mergers, Jay Potter's detailed writings on B&O and CSX operations, Ron Flannery's writings on L&N and Clinchfield, monthly columns in *CTC Board,* Allen Brougham's *Bull Sheet,* and Don Phillips' articles in *TRAINS Magazine* and the *Washington Post* were especially helpful.

Thanks to all the CSX and Conrail employees over the years who have helped me better understand how their railroad does its job. This book is a tribute to everyone who has made CSX what it is today.

Introduction

Modern-day CSX is a vast, complex, intermodal transportation company, and the railroad is the largest component and has the greatest historical interest. It is the railroad, its history, and its operations that is the primary focus of this book. In 2004, CSX's rail operations were the largest and most extensive in the eastern United States. It operates approximately 23,000 miles of line, consists of more than 42,000 track miles, and spans 23 states, the District of Columbia, and Ontario and Quebec in Canada. Within this territory it serves every major urban area with a myriad of lines. These reach from Boston to New Orleans, and Chicago to Miami, and connect hundreds of communities in between. Not only does CSX incorporate America's oldest common carrier railroad, the Baltimore & Ohio, which was chartered in 1827, but its transport heritage dates back to 1785, before the dawn of the railroad age.

CSX local 723 departs Chattanooga, Tennessee, for a 76-mile roundtrip to Dalton, Georgia, on November 15, 1992. This historic trackage traces its origins to 1836 and the Western & Atlantic Railroad, which is unusual because it was built and owned by the State of Georgia. Much of the line was destroyed in Sherman's Atlanta Campaign in 1864. The Nashville, Chattanooga & St. Louis Railway acquired the lease with the W&A properties in 1890, although ownership remained with the state. This lease passed to L&N upon its 1957 merger with NC&St.L, and subsequently to Seaboard System and CSX. ***Scott Muskopf***

CSX's railroad lines are a complex weave of more than a dozen significant twentieth-century railroad companies. The B&O, Chesapeake & Ohio, Louisville & Nashville, Seaboard Air Line, Atlantic Coast Line, and New York Central make up the larger share of its contemporary route structure. CSX also incorporates portions of other smaller, classic railroads such as Clinchfield, Richmond, Fredericksburg & Potomac, Chicago & Eastern Illinois, Monon, Piedmont Northern, Georgia Railroad, Western Railroad of Alabama, and Western Maryland.

This heritage makes for a fascinating study. The vast transportation company that is today's CSX is the amalgam of these varied, geographically diverse, and once independently managed railroads. CSX is neither the sum of these operations, nor is it strictly defined by these historic properties. CSX, as it exists today, is not the result of a single historic grand plan. In the formative days of railroading, lines were typically chartered, built, and operated to benefit local regional economies. Regional concerns, not national or international shipping patterns, dictated how and where lines were located. Anticipated traffic tended to be of a regional and local nature. The B&O was chartered for the benefit of the city of Baltimore. It was conceived in reaction to the opening of New York's Erie Canal and seen as a route that would connect the port of Baltimore with the Ohio River. The Louisville & Nashville was built to connect its two namesake cities. Dozens of small railroads were chartered to improve local transport, advance local businesses, and allow residents in a local region easier overland travel to their neighboring cities and towns.

While these railroads may have participated in the transport of some national or international traffic, local traffic demands, local requirements of charter, and local vision dictated where tracks were located and what towns and cities were served. Likewise, local concerns resulted in the placement of shops, yards, offices, and other facilities. While the demands and role of CSX's lines have changed and evolved greatly since those times, often the location of its routes, if not the precise alignment of its tracks, and the location of support facilities stem from historical precedents dating back to the demands on the original companies.

In the late nineteenth century, local demands gave way to more regional demands. Railroad systems emerged as local lines were joined and routes were extended. The B&O reached well beyond its chartered terminal on the Ohio River, to Chicago and St. Louis. Boston & Worcester and Western were merged to form the Boston & Albany, which later became part of the New York Central, itself the result of connecting numerous short local lines. The L&N extended lines across the Southeast, connecting Memphis, New Orleans, Montgomery, and Cincinnati among other points. Routes along the Atlantic seaboard were joined to form both the Atlantic Coast Line and its competitor, Seaboard Air Line. Lines in Virginia were merged and extended to form the Chesapeake & Ohio. CSX's components fulfilled the visions of great railroad empire builders: J. P. Morgan, the Vanderbilts, C. P. Huntington, and others. By the turn of the twentieth century, railroads had evolved into a national transportation network. In the nineteenth century, the railroad had developed and reigned as the supreme form of transport. It had carried everything from humans and machines, to minerals, merchandise, and produce. Railroads operated in a free market environment, largely unhindered by modal competition, government regulation, or public sentiment. Railroad companies and moguls competed with each other for market share of transportation, and railroad empires and dynasties helped define the business community. During this time, CSX's component companies evolved and established their routes and community presence, and often helped create and develop the towns and places they served.

During the twentieth century, how to best organize, reorganize, control, and competitively operate the American railroad network involved complex machinations of

business and government leaders. The role of the railroad evolved and changed. Increasingly stringent government regulations altered, shaped, directed, and in some cases restrained the way the companies did business. Equally important, new transport modes developed and competed with railroads, ultimately eroding railroad supremacy and forcing them out of many traditional areas of transport.

Traditionally, C&O had trackage rights over the Southern Railway from Orange, Virginia, to reach connections at Washington, D.C. For freight movements, C&O largely utilized these rights to reach Potomac Yard in Alexandria, Virginia. On October 20, 1981, a westward loaded coal train passes the passenger station in Alexandria. In the lead is Chessie System B30-7 No. 8242 sub-lettered for C&O. Following the inclusion of RF&P in the CSX system, trackage rights over the old Southern route became unnecessary and the agreement came to an end in March 1994. ***Doug Eisele***

To satisfy new government requirements for safety, railroads adopted a variety of new technologies that changed the character of trains. To promote their lines and help placate a public increasingly outraged by real and perceived abuses, railroads developed elaborate and colorful advertising campaigns. To better compete with each other and other modes of transportation, railroads improved efficiency that included the operation of longer, heavier, and faster trains. Some of CSX's component railroads were known for their distinctive mastery of twentieth-century railroad efficiency. C&O became an expert coal hauler and operated some of the heaviest trains in the world with the heaviest reciprocating steam locomotives ever built. New York Central refined their steam locomotives to new levels of perfection for both passenger and freight service.

By the time the United States entered World War I, the railroad network had bogged down to such an extent that the federal government took temporary control of the industry. During the 1920s, railroads felt the growing effects of modal competition from motor trucks, automobiles, and water transport. It was competition that government investment mostly subsidized. Modal competition spurred growing interest in consolidation of the railroad industry. Numerous schemes were suggested, from the total unification of the railroads to a variety of regional and systematic groupings of companies. While none of these schemes came to fruition, they produced a few mergers and acquisitions such as B&O's acquisition of the Buffalo, Rochester & Pittsburgh in 1930.

The Great Depression further weakened the railroad industry. Following the unprecedented surge of railroad traffic during World War II, the railroad industry again declined as greatly increased government highway building and the expansion of the airline industry seriously eroded railroad traffic. Passenger traffic, which had been on the decline since World War I, decreased rapidly in the 1950s and 1960s. Various types of lucrative freight traffic such as perishable fruit and vegetables, small packages, and mail traffic was largely lost to the highways. The gradual switch from coal to oil as a heating fuel changed the dynamics of the coal market. Another change was the general decline of heavy industry in the Northeast and new development in the Southeast. These changes altered the traditional traffic patterns and financial positions of American railroads. The northeastern giants were weakened, but southern roads were strengthened. By the late 1950s there was a renewed clamoring within the industry for consolidation.

During the 1960s, many traditional railroad companies merged, including those that eventually produced CSX. The most infamous combination, however, was between Pennsylvania Railroad and New York Central in 1968, which resulted in a catastrophic financial collapse that had profound implications for American railroading. Ultimately, government intervention spawned Amtrak—which forever separated long-distance passenger operations from operation by traditional private companies—and the creation of Conrail from the bankrupt ruins of Penn Central and other eastern carriers. Finally, in 1980, the federal government deregulated the railroads, which helped put a new era of railroad prosperity in motion.

One of the implications of railroad consolidation was the need to eliminate redundancy within the railroad industry. CSX operates far less trackage and employs far fewer people than a comparative sum of its predecessors. Route mileage was trimmed through the consolidation of duplicative routes, abandonment of unproductive lines, and the sale of marginally productive lines to smaller railroads. Line mileage was trimmed by implementing modern technology such as Centralized Traffic Control (CTC), to allow fewer tracks to carry greater capacity. Modern labor agreements combined with labor-saving technology, facility consolidation, and the outsourcing of some railroad jobs have greatly increased railroad worker productivity and allowed for much reduced employment, not just on CSX, but on lines all across the country. Today CSX carries more traffic than ever before. While some lines and yards are hotbeds of activity, others lay abandoned, disused, or function as a shadow of their former glory. It is not clear that all line closures have been in the best long-term benefit for either CSX or the nation. Sometimes lines are shut and lifted simply to satisfy short-term financial objectives, and in the long run, it may have been better to keep them than to close them.

In many ways, the story of CSX is the story of American railroading. The history of CSX is the history of those companies and lines that were assembled into the new system. The operation of trains—some 1,700 per day—is how CSX moves its business. Transportation is its story.

On February 10, 2003, a pair of CSX DASH 8-40CWS leads a northward unit grain train across the Etowah River bridge in Cartersville, Georgia, on the W&A Subdivision. This route was originally the Western and Atlantic Railroad between Atlanta, Georgia, and Chattanooga, Tennessee. The line was made famous by the Great Locomotive Chase of 1862, and leased to L&N predecessor Nashville, Chattanooga, and St. Louis Railway in 1890. The line was built in 1841 through 1850 by the state of Georgia and is now operated by CSX on a long-term lease. *Mark Leppert*

At 10:33 a.m. on November 14, 1948, Baltimore & Ohio Mikado 4445 and Pacific 5085 lead train No. 30 eastbound up the Cranberry Grade at Terra Alta, West Virginia. This is one of the steepest double-track mainlines in the eastern United States. *Bruce Fales, Jay Williams Collection*

CHAPTER ONE

CSX PREDECESSORS

The railroads that have merged to form modern-day CSX each have their own history. This chapter looks at the most important pre-Conrail components of today's CSX. Since 1999, the Conrail predecessors—New York Central, Pennsylvania, Erie Lackawanna, Reading, Central Railroad of New Jersey, and others—also play a role in CSX operations and deserve their own story; however, there is not space in this book to give these fascinating railroads justice. Some of the smaller lines included in CSX are discussed in Chapter 2.

One of Baltimore & Ohio's most famous trains was the *Royal Blue,* which operated between Jersey City and Washington, D.C. This popular train highlighted B&O's influence over Reading and Jersey Central. *Richard Jay Solomon collection*

Baltimore & Ohio

The oldest CSX component, Baltimore & Ohio, was the first American railroad chartered and built as a common carrier, and thus became the prototype for the vast majority of North American railroads. Although it wasn't the first to use steam power, it was the first to adopt the steam locomotive for everyday use, and it was the first to consider using locomotives built in the United States rather than machines imported from Britain.

On February 28, 1827, Baltimore & Ohio was chartered to build from the port city of Baltimore, Maryland, to the Ohio River. The railroad was authorized in response to the recent opening of the Erie Canal across central New York State. This canal directed traffic to and from the interior of the United States to the port of New York, and put other eastern seaboard ports, including Baltimore, at a decided disadvantage. By building a railroad over the mountains to the Ohio River, Baltimore would be in a position to claim a greater share of interior traffic. Although today reaching the Ohio River may seem like a peculiar goal, at the time, the Ohio and Mississippi Rivers and the Great Lakes were the primary means of transport beyond the Appalachians. A great public celebration on July 4, 1828, marked the beginning of construction. Later that year, Baltimore & Ohio's engineers, including Jonathan Knight, William G. McNeill, and George Washington Whistler, traveled to the cradle of railwaydom in Great Britain to study this new form of transport and bring the knowledge and materials necessary back to Baltimore to make the

The National Limited—Along the Potomac River—Baltimore & Ohio Railroad

Baltimore & Ohio's luxurious *National Limited* connected Washington, D.C., and St. Louis. This postcard view from the late steam era depicts the train rolling along the banks of the Potomac River. *Richard Jay Solomon collection*

Baltimore & Ohio's *Capitol Limited,* train No. 5, with P-1d 5048 is at Washington, D.C.'s Union Station at 4:05 p.m. on July 3, 1932. *Bruce Fales, Jay Williams Collection*

B&O work. They were following in the footsteps of Delaware & Hudson's Horatio Allen who had journeyed there earlier in 1828 to bring back rails and locomotives for that line, which at that time was strictly a freight-hauling industrial operation that supplemented inland waterways. The concept of a transport common carrier like the B&O was in its infancy.

B&O's engineers returned to Maryland with hopes of employing steam power. In 1829, Whistler ordered a Stephenson 0-6-0 locomotive from Britain, but the ship carrying the engine sank in the Irish Sea. The first section of line opened to Ellicotts Mills, about 14 miles from Baltimore, and in May 1830, daily horse-drawn passenger service began. Shortly after, Peter Cooper, a successful New York glue maker with investments in the growing port of Baltimore and an interest in mechanics, approached the B&O with a proposal for an American-built locomotive. Peter Cooper publicly demonstrated a diminutive locomotive on August 28, 1830, and successfully hauled 13 tons at 4 miles per hour and reached speeds in excess of 15 miles per hour. This was the first use of an American-built steam locomotive on a common carrier, and it ultimately led to the construction of a fleet of machines derived from its design.

Despite its early start, construction of B&O's line progressed slowly. By 1837, the line had only reached Harpers Ferry, 87 miles from Baltimore. In addition, it had also constructed a 32-mile branch to Washington, D.C. Fourteen years after construction began, the railroad reached Cumberland, Maryland, the eastern terminus of the National Road—an established

On July 27, 1949, Baltimore & Ohio EM-1 7629 ascends the Cranberry Grade at Austin, West Virginia. During World War II, B&O bought EM-1s instead of Electro-Motive FT diesels to comply with War Production Board restrictions. They were B&Os last new freight steam. B&O was fully dieselized less than a decade after this image was made. *Bruce Fales, Jay Williams collection*

trade route over the mountains. West of Cumberland the B&O faced stiff mountain grades and expensive construction. Fortunately, coal mines around Cumberland provided B&O with lucrative business, which by the end of the 1840s had become its dominant traffic. Building west between Keyser and Grafton, West Virginia (then part of Virginia), the railroad engineered its famous Seventeen Mile Grade to the summit at Altamont. This was one of four significant grades that defined operations west of Cumberland, on the line traditionally known as the West End. B&O finally reached the Ohio River at Wheeling, West Virginia, in 1852. A second line to the Ohio, called the Parkersburg Branch, diverged at Grafton, and traveled due west across West Virginia where it reached its namesake in 1857. Later this became part of B&O's route to St. Louis.

Edward Hungerford, in his book *Daniel Willard Rides the Line,* credits John W. Garrett, who managed the line from 1859 to 1884, for bringing the line through the Civil War, when it was subject to raids and ruinous attacks, and overseeing its postwar expansion from just over 500 route miles to more than 1,700 miles. Lines were extended into Ohio from both Wheeling and Parkersburg, and

through lease and acquisition, B&O established through routes to Columbus and the Lake Erie port at Sandusky. Among the most significant extensions was the route northwest from Cumberland into Pennsylvania over Sand Patch to Connellsville and on to Pittsburgh, which B&O reached in 1871. This line was extended across Ohio and Indiana to Chicago by 1874. As B&O and the nation developed, this route became its primary trunk for through traffic. Although unfulfilled, Hungerford indicates that Garrett had visions of extending B&O's influence southward to Atlanta and New Orleans. From a transportation perspective, Garrett's goals were ultimately achieved, albeit more than a century later in the CSX era.

Baltimore & Ohio's *Metropolitan Special*, train No. 12 led by Mikado 4453 and Pacific 5035, works the Cranberry Grade near Austin, West Virginia, on July 27, 1949. B&O's old West End was the mountain grades west of Cumberland, Maryland, on the railroad's original line to Wheeling, West Virginia. In later years this served as the line to St. Louis and as a major coal conduit. *Bruce Fales, Jay Williams Collection*

B&O's expansion put it in a good position to move through traffic, but it lagged behind the nation's two largest railroads, the Pennsylvania and New York Central. During the panic of 1893, B&O's finances faltered, and in 1896, it entered receivership. By 1900, B&O was under control of the Pennsylvania Railroad, which appointed Leonor F. Loree to run B&O. During Loree's administration, B&O improved its freight hauling capacity with the construction of new yards at Connellsville and New Castle, Pennsylvania, which served the railroad into the CSX era. Coal traffic was facilitated with a new yard at Keyser, West Virginia.

B&O was freed from PRR control in the first decade of the twentieth century when antitrust sentiment fought against railroad empire building and rate control. In 1910, Daniel Willard became president of the B&O, a post he held for more than 30 years. Willard is regarded as one of the great railroaders of the twentieth century. He enjoyed a lifelong railroad career and worked his way up through the ranks. Under his expert management, B&O improved its lines by double-tracking most of its Baltimore to Chicago trunk, straightening and realigning its route to reduce the grades and curves, and improving bridges to allow heavier trains and faster speeds. Among Willard's improvements, from which CSX still benefits today, was the Magnolia Cutoff along the Potomac River east of Cumberland. Inspired by the parallel Western Maryland built in 1906, the Magnolia Cutoff was necessary to help relieve congestion on traffic bottlenecks east of Cumberland. Another improvement was construction of a modern double span across the Susquehanna River at Havre de Grace, Maryland, which was engineered by Arthur W. Thompson. This reaches 6,108 feet across the broad waters of the lower Susquehanna River, at a height of 90 feet. Willard's improvements included modernizing the Sand Patch crossing and the construction of a second Kingwood Tunnel on the West End.

B&O, like all American railroads, came under the control of the federal government between 1917 and 1920 when the railroad network had bogged down as a result of greatly increased traffic because of U.S. involvement in World War I. Although the railroads were returned to the private sector in 1920, the years of government control soured railroad management to future government interference in their operations.

In the late 1920s, B&O had visions of putting together a super east-west mainline

A Baltimore & Ohio streamlined passenger train makes an evening stop in suburban Pittsburgh, Pennsylvania. B&O used Pittsburgh & Lake Erie between McKeesport and New Castle Junction to better serve downtown Pittsburgh and to avoid its own steeply graded route through the Pittsburgh area. ***Richard Jay Solomon***

Baltimore & Ohio reached New York City by virtue of its control of the Reading Company, which controlled the Central Railroad of New Jersey. Like other New York–area railroads, B&O used car floats to transport freight cars across the Hudson. After World War I, passengers had the option of bus transport from Jersey City to New York. In July 1964, B&O tug *Howard Simpson* hauls a barge laden with refrigerated boxcars carrying fruit from California. This photo was taken at the end of B&O's car ferry era; service was withdrawn in an effort to cut expenses. *Richard Jay Solomon*

across central Pennsylvania. As a result of these hopes and consolidation schemes, B&O bought the Buffalo, Rochester & Pittsburgh in 1930, and then bought the Buffalo & Susquehanna in 1932. Its grand plans never came to fruition, but the BR&P lines remained part of the B&O empire until the 1980s, while the B&S lines were mostly trimmed in the steam era. During the 1930s, the effects of the Great Depression hit the B&O hard, and while the line faltered, it did not succumb to receivership.

In the 1920s and 1930s, B&O was among America's diesel pioneers. It ordered one of the first Alco-GE-Ingersoll-Rand boxcabs for switching services, and in 1937, it bought the first streamlined diesels not part of a fixed-train set—Electro-Motive Corporation's model EA, which were the very first E units. At the end of the decade, B&O provided EMC with the first road-testing ground for its FT freight diesel. This was the first commercially successful and mass-produced road freight diesel, and B&O was among the EMC's early customers. World War II interfered with B&O's early dieselization plans. While the railroad enjoyed record traffic levels, the War Production Board—a government body that allocated railroad equipment purchases during the war in an effort to control the use of crucial resources needed for the war effort—compelled B&O to purchase modern steam instead of additional FTs. The result was B&O's last freight steam, its

B.&O.C.T.R.R.

The Baltimore & Ohio Chicago Terminal Railroad was B&O's Chicago area subsidiary. On November 22, 1956, a workman checks the journals on a B&OCT switcher. *Jim Shaughnessy*

famous 2-8-8-4 EM1s, which were built by Baldwin. Despite its early efforts, after the war B&O was slower to complete dieselization than other lines. But by the mid-1950s, the vast majority of its operations were diesel powered.

Baltimore & Ohio declined after World War II. The general decline and exodus of heavy industry, the shift from coal to oil as a heating fuel, massive public investment in highway infrastructure, combined with inflexible rate regulation and antiquated labor arrangements contributed to B&O's woes. By the late 1950s, B&O entertained merger plans to help it survive in the changing economy.

Chesapeake & Ohio

Chesapeake & Ohio was formed in 1868 by the merger of Virginia Central and Covington & Ohio. Virginia Central's predecessor, the Louisa Railroad, had been chartered in 1836, and in its early years effectively functioned as a branch of the Richmond, Fredericksburg & Potomac and connected with that line at Hanover Junction (today known as Doswell). Virginia Central assumed operations of the Louisa Railroad in 1850, and with help from the Commonwealth of Virginia, had completed a route over the Blue Ridge to Jackson's

Baltimore & Ohio's last new steam locomotives were its Baldwin-built EM-1 articulateds delivered after World War II. On September 22, 1955, B&O EM-1s prepare to move freight at Fales Spur on the Lake Branch south of Painesville, Ohio. By 1958, B&O, like most American railroads, was 100 percent diesel hauled. *Jim Shaughnessy*

Baltimore & Ohio locomotives rest overnight between assignments at the Ivy City engine house in Washington, D.C., on June 18, 1960. *Jim Shaughnessy*

At 4 p.m. on July 24, 1958, westward Baltimore & Ohio freight No. 91 waits as eastward No. 98, led by a pair of Electro-Motive F units, passes at Sandoval, Illinois. Sandoval is located in central Illinois on the B&O route to St. Louis and was a diamond crossing with the Illinois Central at the time of this photograph. The IC through Sandoval has since been abandoned. *Richard Jay Solomon*

Baltimore & Ohio GP40 4042 leads a westward freight down the west slope of Sand Patch toward Pittsburgh at Garrett, Pennsylvania, on May 11, 1975. In later years, B&O's route from Cumberland, Maryland, to Chicago via Pittsburgh, grew to greater importance than its original mainline west from Cumberland toward Grafton. *Jim Marcus, Doug Eisele collection*

Chesapeake & Ohio operated Budd-built rail diesel cars on its Big Sandy Division between Ashland and Elkhorn City, Kentucky. By the 1950s this line hosted minimal passenger service, and the mainstay of its traffic was, and still is, coal. These RDCs were unusual in that they had room for baggage and the mail and express business, as well as passenger seats and were regularly assigned to daily Big Sandy trains 36 and 39. *Richard Jay Solomon*

River Station (today's Clifton Forge) by 1857. The most difficult portion of this line was the Blue Ridge crossing, which was engineered by Colonel Claudius Crozet and built as the Blue Ridge Railroad. Four tunnels were required, including a very long summit tunnel at Afton. During the Civil War, Virginia Central served as an important route for Confederate forces, and was heavily damaged as a result. By the end of the war the line was in tatters and impassible.

One of the true giants of the steam era was Chesapeake & Ohio's massive 2-6-6-6 Alleghany, one of the largest steam locomotives ever built. On June 26, 1951, Alleghany 1635 leads 140 cars of coal at 20 miles per hour at Montgomery, West Virginia. A single Alleghany was designed to lift 5,750 tons over C&O's mountain grade between Hinton and Clifton Forge. Today, C&O's successor, CSX, moves coal trains weighing up to 20,000 pounds with modern AC4400CW diesels. ***Otto Perry, Denver Public Library Western History Department***

After the war, in 1869, Collis P. Huntington took an interest in the financing and management of C&O. Huntington was one of the "Big Four"—the men responsible for financing and building Central Pacific, the western portion of the first transcontinental railroad. He assumed the presidency of C&O on July 15, 1869, just a little more than two months after the famous golden spike ceremony at Promontory, Utah, which marked the completion of the transcontinental route.

Under Huntington, C&O expanded rapidly. By April 1873, it had connected a 428-mile route that reached from Richmond to the Ohio

Chesapeake & Ohio's eastward *F.F.V.*, train No. 6, takes mail during its scheduled station stop at Kenova, West Virginia. *F.F.V.* stood for "Fast Flying Virginian" and operated daily, connecting Cincinnati; Washington, D.C.; and New York City. The bridge over the top of the C&O carries the Norfolk & Western mainline. Compare this view at Kenova with the under and over view at Kenova by Marshall Beecher in Chapter 2. *Richard Jay Solomon*

The Chesapeake & Ohio herald on one of its streamlined Hudson-type steam locomotives. Synonymous with coal, C&O was among the last railroads to purchase new steam power. *Brian Solomon*

River, at a new town named Huntington, West Virginia. Additional lines were built to tap the coal-rich area of central Appalachia, an area later known as the "Coal Bin." Through connecting lines, C&O reached Cincinnati in 1881. C. P. Huntington built a strategic route east from Richmond to the tidewater port of Newport News, Virginia, and this developed into a significant coal conduit. By the time this route opened to traffic in 1882, coal was becoming C&O's primary traffic source. Despite C&O's strategic location and traffic potential, the line faltered under Huntington's administration, and his hopes for a true transcontinental transportation scheme ended in 1888 when Vanderbilt interests, backed by Drexel, Morgan & Company, assumed control of C&O. The Vanderbilts were known for their dynamic railroad empire based on the

New York Central & Hudson River Railroad (which eventually became the New York Central System). Under Vanderbilt control and with adequate financing, C&O continued to build and acquire key routes.

One of C&O's strategic acquisitions was the Richmond & Alleghany railroad, which had been built on a low-grade route following the old James River Company canal. The James River Co. was among America's earliest transportation companies. It was founded in 1785, and famous for having George Washington as its first president. By the early 1880s, the canal was defunct and the railroad was built along its tow path. This line avoids the difficult climb over the Blue Ridge and provides a superior route for the movement of coal bound for Newport News. At approximately the same time as the R&A acquisition, C&O also secured trackage rights over the Southern Railway route to Washington, D.C.

At the turn of the twentieth century, C&O had assembled an enviable railroad network that reached from Newport News and Washington, D.C., to Cincinnati and Louisville. Coal accounted for roughly 50 percent of its traffic and revenue. The nation's two largest railroads, New York Central and Pennsylvania, had both gained partial control of the line. Control was severed in 1908, however, as a result of the trust-busting backlash of the period.

C&O continued to expand its influence. In 1903, it became part owner of the Hocking Valley Railroad, a strategic line that reached from the Ohio River city of Gallipolis, Ohio, to Toledo. Initially, C&O did not connect directly with the Hocking Valley, and it used various lines to reach this important trackage. Ultimately, C&O built a route called the C&O Northern Line to connect Waverly and Columbus, Ohio, which provided its own all-rail link to Lake Erie. C&O further

Following the collapse of an anticipated merger between C&O, Wheeling & Lake Erie, Nickel Plate Road, and Pere Marquette, C&O bought the Pere Marquette in 1947. This allowed C&O to expand beyond its traditional area—giving it a through route from Chicago to Detroit and Buffalo, as well as extensive trackage in lower Michigan. On September 10, 1972, a C&O GP35 leads a freight at Grand Rapids, Michigan. ***R.R. Richardson, Doug Eisele collection***

A quintet of C&O GP9s lead a coal train downgrade of the Blue Ridge at Ivy, Virginia, on the North Mountain Subdivision, destined for interchange with the RF&P at Doswell. This was an experimental routing that didn't last very long. Because of difficult grades on two mountain summits on this route, the vast majority of eastward coal traveled via the James River Subdivision. *Jeremy F. Plant*

cemented its western connections in 1910 with the acquisition of the Chicago, Cincinnati & Louisville, which provided a direct link to Chicago. By 1911, C&O had bought control of the Hocking Valley. Despite the strategic Chicago connection, C&O's Hocking Valley trackage to Lake Erie proved to be a more valuable route for hauling coal. In fact, in later years, C&O's Chicago line was little more than a passenger route. Early in the CSX era, most of the route west of Cincinnati was downgraded or abandoned.

In 1923, Oris P. and Mantis J. Van Sweringen bought control of the line. The Van Sweringen brothers were eccentric bachelors from Cleveland who, starting in 1916, assembled an impressive railroad empire using cleverly organized and tenuously balanced financing. First they took control of the Nickel Plate Road, and by the early 1930s, they controlled C&O, Pere Marquette, Erie Railroad, Wheeling & Lake Erie, Missouri Pacific, and Chicago & Eastern Illinois. From 1929, NKP, C&O, PM, Erie, and W&LE were under the umbrella of the Van Sweringens' Alleghany Corporation, which takes its name from C&O's mainline summit. Efforts to merge the lines were unsuccessful, but one of their more famous endeavors resulted in the construction of Cleveland Union Terminal and the Shaker Heights Rapid Transit system that served the new upscale Cleveland suburb of that name. Today SHRT is an integral part of the Cleveland rail transit network.

The onset of the Great Depression unraveled the Van Sweringen empire. Following their deaths in 1935 and 1936, financial wizard Robert Young took control of the Alleghany railroads. Like the Van Sweringens, he tried to merge the lines without success. In 1942, he became chairman of C&O, and in 1947, merged C&O and Pere Marquette (which connected Chicago, Detroit, and Buffalo via Ontario, and operated a substantial network of Michigan trackage, including Lake Michigan car ferries). Young then sold

In the 1950s, six-motor diesels were an anomaly in daily operations. A pair of Baldwin AS-616s grind past the tower at Covington, Kentucky, with a long cut of coal hoppers on July 28, 1958. Where these six-motor diesels were unusual, today's modern six-motor diesels are standard power on CSX, and pairs of AC4400CWs are now typically used to haul coal trains. Modern six-motor diesels are significantly more powerful, reliable, and fuel efficient than these old Baldwins. *Richard Jay Solomon*

Both Seaboard Air Line and Atlantic Coast Line operated intensive, long-distance passenger services connecting Northeast cities with resort communities in Florida and Georgia. On September 5, 1970, the last full year of private passenger operations before the formation of Amtrak, Seaboard Coast Line's train No. 75, the *Gulf Coast Special,* passes Charleston, South Carolina, on the old ACL route. *George Kowanski*

his interests in Nickel Plate Road and W&LE and hoped to combine C&O with New York Central. He left C&O in 1954 to focus on the New York Central, but was unable to merge the two lines. By the mid-1950s, C&O was one of the most prosperous railroads in the United States. Its excellent modern infrastructure, characterized by immaculate rights-of-way, heavy rail, and modern, color-light signaling was largely a result of heavy investment and planning during the Van Sweringen and Young administrations.

Atlantic Coast Line

The devastation of the Civil War had left many railroads, from southern Virginia to Georgia, in poor physical and financial condition. After the war, Northern business entrepreneurs took advantage of this situation and consolidated railroad systems from a myriad of local and regional lines. One of the strongest postwar southern networks to evolve was the Atlantic Coast Line, which reached from Richmond, Virginia, to Charleston, South Carolina. Among its significant components were Virginia's Petersburg Railroad, which had been chartered in 1830; North Carolina's Wilmington & Weldon Railroad; and the Wilmington & Manchester Railroad. "Atlantic Coast Line" was first used as a marketing name in the 1870s. Under the direction of Baltimore financier William T. Walters, the ACL coalesced, and was consolidated as the Atlantic Coast Line Company by 1893. Following Walters' death in 1894, his son, Henry, continued the consolidation. By 1900, the consolidated lines consisted of approximately 2,000 route miles. ACL now reached from Richmond to Charleston and Augusta, Georgia. The year 1902 was important for ACL. It absorbed its friendly southern connection, a 2,100-mile network put together by Henry B. Plant during the previous decades that reached across Florida, Georgia, and South Carolina. Also that year, ACL acquired majority interest in the Louisville & Nashville, although it did not move to exercise direct control at that time.

Atlantic Coast Line continued to improve its route structure by building and acquiring lines in Florida, and taking control of the weakly financed Atlanta, Birmingham & Atlantic in the 1920s, which formally merged with the ACL in 1945. On the eve of World War I, ACL was considered one of the strongest railways in the South with more than 4,500 route miles.

ACL thrived on perishable traffic moving from Florida and Georgia to northern cities. Traditionally, fruits and vegetables traveled in insulated boxcars chilled with blocks of ice. ACL and its competitor, Seaboard Air Line, fostered winter resort development in Florida and southern coastal cities. Relatively fast passenger service created seasonal tourism and passenger traffic, and remained heavy on these north-south routes through the advent of Amtrak in 1971.

Fast freight and heavy passenger traffic led ACL to double-track much of its Richmond-Jacksonville trunk route and equip the line with automatic block signals to add capacity and improve safety. Following World War II, ACL was quick to invest in CTC, and its lines were a showcase for modern signaling. It dieselized rapidly, and by 1954, had operated its last

On September 3, 1970, Seaboard Coast Line train No. 86, the northward *Everglades*, makes a station stop at Broad Street Station in Richmond, Virginia. Prior to the 1967 Seaboard Coast Line merger, passenger trains of both component lines used the Richmond, Fredericksburg & Potomac to reach Washington, D.C. Today, while Amtrak serves two stations in Richmond, the old Broad Street Station is now a science museum. *George Kowanski*

revenue steam power. Although most of Atlantic Coast Line's routes enjoyed low-grade profiles, ACL's Charleston & Western Carolina subsidiary faced some tough grades on its run to Spartanburg, South Carolina, where it connected with an ACL affiliate, the Clinchfield. C&WC reached from the coastal city of Port Royal, South Carolina, to Spartanburg via Augusta, Georgia.

Traditionally, ACL's corporate headquarters was located in Wilmington, North Carolina, but it was relocated to Jacksonville, Florida, in 1960. Since that time, Jacksonville has played a greater importance as both a business and operational center for ACL and today for CSX.

The northward flow of traffic made Richmond ACL's most important interchange point. Much of ACL's freight and passenger traffic was forwarded north from Richmond over the Richmond, Fredericksburg & Potomac, which ACL partly owned.

From the 1920s onward, increasing highway competition eroded ACL's market share of traditional traffic flows, most significantly its prized perishable traffic. By the 1950s, ACL and its north-south rival, Seaboard Air Line, were discussing a merger to reduce costs and more effectively compete with non-rail modes. Finally after a decade of discussion and regulatory hurdles, ACL and Seaboard merged in 1967, and became the Seaboard Coast Line. This merger was one of the more significant moves that ultimately led to the formation of CSX.

Seaboard Air Line Railroad

As in the case of its chief competitor, Atlantic Coast Line, the Seaboard Air Line was a system pieced together by Northern business interests in the wake of the Civil War, and it didn't take its modern form until the early twentieth century. SAL's earliest component was the line between Weldon, North Carolina, and Portsmouth, Virginia, which dated to the formative days of American railroading. This route opened in 1834, four years after B&O's pioneering line. During the 1870s and 1880s, Baltimore business-mogul John M. Robinson assembled a network of railroads, including the Seaboard & Roanoke; Raleigh & Augusta Air Line; Raleigh & Gaston; Carolina Central; and Georgia, Carolina & Northern. By 1892, this network formed a northeast-southwest spine connecting Portsmouth with Atlanta and was collectively known as the Seaboard Air Line System. This name was used a full decade before the Wright brothers put Kitty Hawk on the map with their magnificent flying machine—in those days an "air line" referred to a railroad's relatively tangent profile.

In the late 1890s, under new management, the railroad expanded significantly when combined with Georgia & Alabama; Florida Central & Peninsular; and the newly built Richmond, Petersburg & Carolina. During this time, the railroad organized the flow of its northerly traffic using Richmond, Fredericksburg & Potomac north of Richmond. In 1900, the railroad's corporate structure was simplified, and most of the constituent railroads merged to form the Seaboard Air Line Railway. The construction of a crucial 90-mile link between Cheraw and Columbia, South Carolina, gave the Seaboard its principal north-south line that ran from Richmond to Jacksonville. This allowed the southern North Carolina town of Hamlet to develop as the operational focal point of its system. Here SAL's primary east-west routes intersected its north-south lines. SAL competed with both the Atlantic Coast Line and Southern Railway. Unlike the ACL, however, Seaboard's inland routes were plagued with a difficult hill-and-dale grade profile that was expensive to operate. In its early years, SAL was financially weak, but it continued expansion in the first decades of the twentieth century. It reached the growing industrial center of Birmingham, but entered receivership in 1908. In 1915, the Seaboard was again restructured and adopted the name Seaboard

Air Line Railroad. With improved finances, it continued vigorous expansion into the 1920s and built a network across Florida, from the panhandle city of Tallahassee to Jacksonville, with mainlines to Tampa, St. Petersburg, West Palm Beach, and Miami. As a result, it flourished in the 1920s, but sank again with the onset of the Great Depression. It wasn't until after World War II that the SAL, under the direction of John Walter Smith, enjoyed prosperity. It completed mainline dieselization by 1953, and installed cost-saving CTC signaling across most of its system. Smith led the Seaboard to the merger with the ACL.

Today the Seaboard Air Line is less well known than its most famous passenger train, the legendary *Orange Blossom Special,* a deluxe sleeping car run that began in 1925 and carried passengers to Florida. In 1939, Seaboard was the first railroad in the South to introduce a diesel streamliner, the *Silver Meteor*, which ran overnight between New York and Miami, with a section that went to St. Petersburg. In 1954, this luxurious train averaged 54 miles per hour on its 24-hour run to Miami.

Although less prominent to the public than its famous passenger trains, Seaboard's lucrative freight traffic was of greater importance to its stockholders. Like the ACL, it whisked perishables northward. As southern industry flourished after World War II, SAL carried an increasing amount of manufactured products. Phosphate traffic and timber products were also important.

Seaboard's insignia included a stylized heart, inscribed in block capital letters,

Seaboard Air Line and Atlantic Coast Line merged in 1967 to form Seaboard Coast Line. On August 10, 1971, a former SAL Alco RS-3 lettered for its new owner rests with a caboose in Clearwater, Florida. ***R.R. Richardson, Doug Eisele collection***

"Through the heart of the South." The line reached from Richmond and Portsmouth via Hamlet to Birmingham, Alabama; Charleston, South Carolina; Savannah, Georgia; and across Florida. It also had a line to Montgomery, Alabama; via Abbeyville to Richland, Georgia; and a tangent route from Hamlet to Wilmington, North Carolina. The "S" in today's CSX stems from the Seaboard legacy.

Louisville & Nashville Alco FA diesels lead a freight at Louisville, Kentucky, in the mid-1960s. L&N purchased large numbers of Alco products and was one of the last Class 1 carriers to maintain a sizable Alco fleet; some 1960s-era Century units survived into the 1980s. Note the traditional switch lanterns. *Robert J. Doherty*

Louisville & Nashville

During most of its existence as an independently managed railroad, Louisville & Nashville was the "Old Reliable." Chartered in 1850 to connect its namesake cities, Maury Klein, in his *History of the Louisville & Nashville Railroad*, deemes the railroad the "biggest and most ambitious project in Kentucky history," and explains that the root interest in constructing the line stemmed from the heated rivalry of these two cities. Perhaps equally important was Louisville's role as an Ohio River shipping center. Louisville hoped the L&N would help funnel trade and give it an edge over other Ohio river cities, especially Cincinnati.

L&N was built to 5-foot gauge, as that was the most common track width in Kentucky and was standard throughout most of the South at the time. In its formative years, L&N progressed slowly. It was surveyed in 1851, and the first rails were laid in 1853. Under the new leadership of James Guthrie and Albert Fink, L&N achieved its goal and the 185-mile line was finally completed in autumn 1859. Special trains operated over the length of the line in October, and regular services commenced on Halloween. Within a year, work had begun on a second line that ultimately reached Memphis.

Brand-new Louisville & Nashville F7 diesels lead a long freight near Louisville, Kentucky, in June 1950. L&N, as with most American railroads, invested heavily in diesels after World War II. These F7s were typical of its first-generation diesels; L&N had more than 200 F units on its roster. *Otto Perry, Denver Public Library Western History Department*

L&N's north-south alignment put it in an unusual and precarious situation during the American Civil War that erupted in April 1861. Historians have documented the role of the railroads during the war, with the Union Army's mastery of railroads often credited as a major contributing element to the North's victory over the South in 1865. It is reasonable to say L&N provided a significant part in the war. While attempting to maintain a position of neutrality, L&N variously provided valued transport to both the Confederacy and the Union. Ultimately, it aided the Union forces to a much greater extent. Early in the war, L&N suffered extensive damage from Confederate raiders and those sympathetic to the Confederate cause. Stewart H. Holbrook, in *The Story of American Railroads,* illustrates how General John Hunt Morgan initiated a series of raids on L&N and sabotaged the line by ripping up tracks and destroying freight cars, bridges, culverts, and telegraph lines.

The Civil War was a two-edged sword for L&N; despite destruction the railroad prospered from the volume of traffic moving across its lines. The war was a focal point in the line's early history that ultimately helped paved the way for its future prosperity. After the war, L&N was in an envious position. Unlike most southern railways that lay in ruins, L&N was in relatively good shape. Klein explains that Albert Fink planned an ambitious expansion strategy, which along with economic changes as a result of the war, elevated L&N from a localized carrier to a regional transportation dynamo. Since other healthy railroads already dominated the territory to L&N's north and east, L&N expanded southward, rapidly

The Chicago & Eastern Illinois was a medium-sized Midwestern line that bridged Missouri Pacific and Louisville & Nashville traffic to Chicago. In the late 1960s, the MoPac and L&N effectively divided the C&EI with L&N getting the Evansville, Indiana, to Woodland, Illinois, section that included trackage rights between Woodland Junction and Chicago. On June 29, 1950, a 14-car C&EI local freight at Vincennes, Indiana, follows No. 202, the line's unique BL1, which preceded the more common BL2—GM's early attempt at a road-switcher. *Otto Perry, Denver Public Library Western History Department*

dominated its territory, and ultimately became one of the foremost southern carriers. Expansion was accomplished through purchase, lease, and control of existing lines, as well as through new construction. By 1872, L&N had reached Montgomery, Alabama, and by 1880, it connected the strategic Gulf ports at Pensacola, Florida; Mobile, Alabama; and New Orleans, Louisiana. It had also cemented connections to important gateways at St. Louis, Evansville, and Cincinnati in 1881. In 1883, it connected Louisville and Knoxville, and developed a route across the Florida panhandle. The railroad is credited for the development of the post–Civil War Alabama metropolis of Birmingham. The location of vast iron and coal ores in the region made this location ideally suited as an industrial center. The railroad's penetration of the eastern Kentucky coal fields, first reached with the acquisition of Kentucky Central's lines from Covington to Livingston, was also significant. Although coal represented just a small portion of L&N's traffic in the 1880s, over the succeeding decades, the development of the Kentucky coal fields played an increasingly important role in L&N's fortunes.

In addition to the lines it operated under its own name, L&N bought control of the Nashville, Chattanooga & St. Louis, one of its chief rivals in the region, in 1879. This line maintained independent operation until 1957. It provided L&N with valuable connections, including the Western & Atlantic route to Atlanta—famous for the Great Train Chase initiated by the Andrew's Raiders during the Civil War using the locomotive *General*.

L&N's rapid expansion came at a price. By taking on debt for line acquisition and new construction, the railroad sacrificed local control, and ownership shifted from Louisville to New York. From the last decades of the nineteenth century into the first part of the twentieth century, L&N prospered under the leadership of Milton H. Smith, president from 1884 to 1886 and 1891 to his death in 1921. His influence greatly shaped L&N's business philosophy. He was deeply committed to development of freight traffic. Among the significant events of the Smith regime was the conversion of the railroad from broad gauge to the national 4-foot, 8 1/2-inch standard gauge in 1886.

At the turn of the twentieth century, L&N celebrated its 50th anniversary. It was already a well-established name in American railroading. Its 5,000-mile network blanketed Kentucky, Tennessee, and Alabama, and reached nearly every major gateway in its region. In 1902, the Atlantic Coast Line bought majority interest in the L&N, but little changed. Smith remained in command and the railroad continued its expansion. Among his more ambitious twentieth-century projects was the construction during 1902 to 1907 of a second north-south mainline that connected the gateway cities of Cincinnati and Atlanta and bisected eastern Tennessee via Knoxville.

In the early twentieth century, L&N continued to grow its coal business. It built a myriad of new lines in the eastern Kentucky coal fields in the years immediately prior to World War I and developed major coal terminals at Corbin, Loyall, Ravenna, and Covington, among other places. Coal hoppers gathered from the mines were sorted at these terminals and routed to their respective destinations.

L&N was an atypical American railroad in that it continued to extend its mileage until the onset of the Great Depression. According

Chicago & Eastern Illinois had traditionally cooperated with Louisville & Nashville, Atlantic Coast Line, and other southern lines in the operation of through Chicago to Florida passenger services. On August 8, 1947, a new C&EI E7A leads a Budd-built streamliner southward near the 21st Street Bridge in Chicago. C&EI served Chicago's Dearborn Street Station. ***J. R. Quinn collection***

In July 1958, Louisville & Nashville E and F units lay over at Louisville, Kentucky. L&N regularly assigned Electro-Motive E units to its long-distance passenger services. Locomotive 774 is a prewar E6 that featured a more steeply slanting nose than postwar E-models. *Richard Jay Solomon*

The Monon's route map formed a gigantic letter "X" across Indiana. The railroad replaced steam with Electro-Motive and Alco-GE diesels. A Monon Alco RS-3 switches as a steam hauls Pennsylvania Railroad freight charges across the diamond crossing with the Monon at Limedale, Indiana. In modern times, the PRR line has been abandoned, while the Monon segment functions as a CSX branch to Cloverdale, Indiana. *Richard Jay Solomon collection*

to author Maury Klein, the system reached its steam-era zenith in 1931 with 5,266 route miles. During the Depression, as with all American railroads, L&N's traffic declined dramatically and it began retrenchment.

Since coal was the railroad's lifeblood, it was not an early convert to total diesel power. In 1940, the railroad hauled 31.5 million tons of bituminous coal, more than 10 percent of all bituminous carried by the American railroad network. In 1939, on the eve of World War II, L&N bought its first diesel switchers. During the war, L&N's traffic surged, as did all railroads'. After the war, the railroad modernized its system to meet America's rapidly changing transport demands. It introduced streamlined passenger trains, *The Humming Bird* and the St. Louis-Atlanta *Georgian* in 1949. It also committed to full dieselization that year. Its last fires were dumped in 1957. Large-scale introduction of Centralized Traffic Control to ease movements on its mainlines and building large, modern freight yards were among other improvements. On its 100th anniversary, L&N had 4,780 route miles.

In 1957, L&N merged with its long-time affiliate, the Nashville, Chattanooga & St. Louis. Some observers declared this the first modern railroad merger. Others viewed it as more of a consolidation of L&N's holdings than a major merger. The NC&St.L added 1,043 route miles to L&N's map, providing it with a direct Chattanooga to Atlanta link over the old Western & Atlantic route. Interestingly, the L&N dropped its long-held "Old Reliable" moniker in favor of NC&St.L's "Dixie Line." Regardless of how the L&N/NC&St.L merger is categorized, larger and more significant consolidations happened over the next 25 years that first added to L&N's map, and later blotted out the L&N name from the American railroad map. Today, L&N's route structure is a key component to CSX. It is arguably the most complete of CSX's major constituent lines with virtually all its major routes intact.

Clinchfield

The Clinchfield was about coal. This modern north-south Appalachian line was built to exceptionally high standards, and thus was unlike any other railroad in the eastern United States. Its origins dated to 1886, when various schemes were projected to tap coal fields in Virginia and eastern Kentucky; but things were stalled before completion due to lack of finances. The twentieth-century Clinchfield came about in 1908 when George L. Carter picked up pieces of earlier lines in 1902 and consolidated them as the Carolina, Clinchfield & Ohio. By October 1909, the railroad reached from Dante, Virginia, to Spartanburg, South Carolina. Clinchfield's predecessors, however, had laid out steep, tortuous, and poorly engineered lines.

Clinchfield traversed especially rugged terrain and modernization required great investment for construction of numerous bridges and tunnels. Under Carter's administration the Clinchfield was rebuilt and realigned with reduced gradients and curvature to highly engineered standards. When completed, the maximum southward grade was limited to just 1.5 percent, and the northward grade to 1.7 percent. To reach a connection with the Chesapeake & Ohio, Carter extended the Clinchfield's line 35 miles northward from Dante at Elkhorn City, Kentucky. This route featured among the most difficult construction and required 20 tunnels totaling almost 4 miles and representing more than 10 percent of the new construction line mileage. This extension has a short section of 1.8 percent grade at the mouth of the 7,854-foot-long Sandy Ridge tunnel, the steepest portion of mainline on the Clinchfield route. The Elkhorn City extension opened in February 1915, and this point ultimately developed as the Clinchfield's most important interchange. Other important traditional interchange points were located at St. Paul, Virginia, with Norfolk & Western; Miller Yard, Virginia, with Louisville & Nashville and a regional line called the Interstate; Johnson

The coal-hauling Clinchfield Railroad ran from Elkhorn City, Kentucky, to Spartanburg, South Carolina. It was jointly owned by Louisville & Nashville and Atlantic Coast Line. In July 1968, a southward Clinchfield freight passes St. Paul, Virginia. Four of Clinchfield's F units survived until the CSX-era and regularly worked executive passenger trains. This F7A was not one of the fortunate four and was traded back to EMD in 1974 as credit for new SD45-2s. *Jeremy F. Plant*

City, Tennessee, with the Southern Railway; Bostic, North Carolina, with the Seaboard Air Line; and with both Southern and Atlantic Coast Lines at its southern terminal in Spartanburg, South Carolina.

The strategic nature of the Clinchfield and its lucrative coal traffic made it a profitable and desirable property. In 1924, the Atlantic Coast Line and Louisville & Nashville received regulatory approval to jointly lease the Clinchfield for 999 years. In 1952, the Clinchfield operated 317 miles of line, and 277 of that was its Elkhorn City–Spartanburg mainline. There are four substantial mountain crossings. The most spectacular is at Alta Pass, North Carolina, where the railroad uses a series of reverse curves to ascend a summit 2,620 feet above sea level. In total, the route passes through 54 tunnels. The Clinchfield maintained independent operation into the 1970s, and like other ACL and L&N properties was a component of the Family Lines. It was melded into CSX's Seaboard System at the end of 1982.

Georgia Railroad and West Point Route

Among CSX's components were three affiliated railroads that operated a through route via Atlanta between Augusta, Georgia, and Selma, Alabama.

Georgia Railroad was among CSX's oldest predecessors. It was chartered in December 1833, and construction began at Augusta in 1835. Ultimately, it built a 171-mile line that connected Augusta with Atlanta. In 1836, the company adopted the name Georgia Railroad and Banking Company.

In 1843, the Montgomery and West Point Rail Road Company was formed from the Montgomery Rail Road—an older company that dated from 1834. This line was closely affiliated with Western Rail Road Company of Alabama, and the two lines were

merged on September 1, 1870. In later years it was known as the Western Railway of Alabama and operated an 88-mile line from a connection with the Atlantic & West Point Rail Road at West Point, Georgia, to Montgomery, and beyond to Selma, Alabama.

The Atlanta & West Point Rail Road Company dated from December 1857, when it assumed operations of the 87-mile line between its namesake points. Construction of this route began in 1849 under the stewardship of the Atlanta & La Grange.

Together, the Atlanta & West Point and Western Railway of Alabama operated as the West Point Route. In later years, these lines were under common management with the Georgia Railroad, which itself was operating agent of the Georgia Railroad and Banking Company. Atlantic Coast Line and Louisville & Nashville were both part owners of Georgia Railroad and Banking Company.

Most of the Augusta–Atlanta–Montgomery line was protected by block signals. In 1954, the top speed on the Georgia Railroad was 55 miles per hour for passenger trains, and the West Point Route allowed 65 miles per hour for passenger trains. Both lines had 45-mile-per-hour top speed for freight. These lines did not purchase new steam power after the onset of the Great Depression. After World War II, they made the transition to diesel power with Electro-Motive locomotives. Steam operations ended in 1954.

The merger of Atlantic Coast Line and Seaboard Air Line, followed by increased ownership of L&N by Seaboard Coast Line, brought the Georgia Railroad properties closer into the SCL fold. In 1972, they were logically included in the Family Lines marketing affiliation and became part of the Seaboard System at the end of 1982.

Western Railway of Alabama 4-6-0 No. 175 simmers at Montgomery, Alabama, on October 16, 1929. This locomotive was built by Alco component Rogers in 1900. The Western Railroad of Alabama, along with the Atlanta & West Point, were components of the West Point Route. These lines, along with their affiliate, the Georgia Railroad, are components of the modern-day CSX. Note the West Point Route diamond herald on the cab of the locomotive. ***Otto Perry, Denver Public Library Western History Department***

In the 1970s, the brightly colored Chessie System image prevailed over the more conservative image that B&O and C&O used. The Chessie cat, a traditional symbol of the C&O, became the company's official emblem. On March 17, 1977, a pair of Chessie-painted B&O GP40s lead a mile or more of empty coal hoppers west at Harpers Ferry, West Virginia, on the B&O mainline. These cars continued west of Cumberland on the old West End via Keyser to Grafton, West Virginia. *George Kowanski*

CHAPTER TWO

THE RISE OF CSX

Merger Mania

In November 1957, the two traditional titans of American railroading, New York Central and Pennsylvania Railroads, announced they were contemplating a merger. These lines were the largest, busiest, and most powerful railroads in the country, but they were also in deep financial trouble. Consolidation was considered out of desperation and represented retrenchment. By joining forces, they envisioned being able to survive by cutting duplicative or redundant costs. By 1959, merger talks had stalled and the PRR/NYC combination was called off for awhile. By actively pursuing a potential merger, however, they had pushed the industry toward consolidation, and a variety of different merger schemes were being discussed.

Cando and Bando

The Baltimore & Ohio had suffered from the decline of heavy industry, the shrinking railroad industry, and the effects of intensive government-sponsored road building. B&O was hit especially hard by the recession of 1957, and its management desperately sought a solution to keep the line solvent. By contrast, C&O was one of the few truly prosperous railroads in the East. Its traffic was robust, the flow of bituminous coal from the Pocahontas region, the lucrative automobile traffic in Michigan, and other highly profitable business made for good profits. Coal represented more than 56 percent of C&O revenues. Unlike some traditional railroad traffic, C&O's coal business had not suffered from competition from other modes. Also, unlike most northeastern lines, C&O was not saddled with intensive and costly terminal operations or loss-making commuter passenger services. According to Stephen Salisbury in *No Way to Run a Railroad,* C&O was one of the most profitable railroads in the United States in 1956. Strong companies attract talented people, and C&O had one of the best talent pools in the industry.

Following the PRR/NYC announcement, B&O's president Howard Simpson suggested pairing up with C&O. Merger chatter was just beginning to heat up. When NYC spurned PRR in 1959, Simpson initiated discussions with C&O's Walter Tuohy and Central's Al Perlman to consider a three-way merger. C&O frowned at New York Central, but gladly entertained the B&O. By controlling

In July 1988, a westward freight departs New Castle, Pennsylvania, behind a former C&O GP40, wearing Chessie System paint but renumbered for CSXT. ***Brian Solomon***

Above: A northward freight eases through heavy fog on the old C&O a few miles geographically north of Fostoria, Ohio. Soon the fog will lift and a bright and sunny June day will prevail. *Brian Solomon*

Left: Fostoria, Ohio, is one of the busiest railway junctions in the United States and is a strategic point on CSX. The entire town is crisscrossed by railway tracks. The old B&O mainline to Chicago crosses the old C&O main to Toledo at grade at F tower. Connecting tracks allow trains to diverge in any direction. In addition, both lines cross Norfolk Southern's former Nickel Plate Road mainline. On June 4, 2004, a CSX freight rolls eastward on the old B&O line toward Willard, Ohio. *Brian Solomon*

B&O, C&O could double its territory and diversify its traffic base. Also, as Richard Saunders explains in *Merging Lines: American Railroads 1900–1970,* B&O's debt would offset C&O's tax payments, while B&O might benefit from C&O's strong financial position and its progressive management.

So how did this relate to NYC? Al Perlman remained keen on the prospect of a three-way plan. The root of a C&O–New York Central combination was not a new idea. A decade earlier, Robert Young had made a daring effort to merge the two lines. When the ICC foiled Young's plans, he resigned from C&O and took

over New York Central. Young hired Perlman to run the Central in 1954. When New York Central faltered in 1957, Young had again proposed the C&O–NYC combination, but this time it was C&O that got cold feet. With New York Central's fortunes waning, the PRR-NYC proposal was introduced. Young's dreams ended with his suicide in January 1958.

In June 1960, ignoring Central's plight, C&O sought ICC approval to buy control of B&O. Perlman refused to be left out and continued to push for a three-way merger. C&O and B&O management were hesitant to take on Central because of its precarious financial situation and heavy passenger burden. When Perlman found out that he was frozen out of

friendly merger talks, he waged a proxy fight over B&O and pursued legal battles to be included in C&O/B&O. He was fighting a losing battle.

According to Salisbury, the crucial event that shaped the redrawing of the eastern rail map was a meeting in 1961 at C&O's plush Greenbrier Hotel in White Sulphur Springs, where C&O's Walter Tuohy and John Kusik met with PRR's Jim Symes, David Bevan, and Fred Carpi. Their new vision of the East saw C&O controlling B&O, while PRR would divest its holdings in both Norfolk & Western (also a prosperous coal hauler) and Wabash in order to pave the way for the mother of all mergers: PRR and New York Central. Salisbury writes, "The White Sulphur Springs accord was momentous." Al Perlman was absent.

This set the stage for both the C&O/B&O combination and the N&W, Nickel Plate, and Wabash merger of 1964. At the time, the latter combination may have seemed incongruous since N&W and Nickel Plate didn't even connect. Saunders explains, "The real substance of who could merge and who could not lay below the waterline, so to speak; it was a matter of how deeply a railroad was in debt and what bond issues were coming due, not what dots [on the map] it connected." Unlike the consolidation schemes of the 1920s, these merger plans were drawn up by railroads to satisfy current business needs. C&O was especially hostile to further meddling in its merger plans. C&O's Vice President Owen Clarke was quoted in *TRAINS Magazine* in June 1961: "Compulsory consolidation, in my opinion, is only one step removed from nationalization." Railroad nationalization was an anathema, to suggest it was akin to suggesting communism. In a world dominated by Cold War politics, nationalization talk was a betrayal of the railroads to the enemy. B&O's Jervis Langdon Jr., president of B&O between 1961 and 1965, pointed out in a July 1989 editorial in *TRAINS Magazine* that Perlman's three-way merger goal would have avoided the creation of Penn Central, as presumably PRR would have merged with its natural partners, N&W and Wabash.

Seemingly defeated by events outside his realm of influence, Perlman expressed his opposition to C&O/B&O without NYC, but was soon talking merger with PRR again.

Kenova, West Virginia, is still an important point on the old C&O mainline. In March 2004, an eastward CSX freight holds at the home signal as a Norfolk Southern freight rolls by on the bridge in the background. The lead loco is fresh out of CSX's Huntington, West Virginia, shops and is on its initial shakedown run. The CSX train has just crossed into West Virginia from Kentucky. With the split up of Conrail in 1999, CSX and NS were the two primary railroads in the eastern United States. ***Marshall W. Beecher***

Right: Western Maryland was a medium-sized coal hauler that operated west from Baltimore to Cumberland with mainlines to Connellsville, Pennsylvania, and Elkins, West Virginia. One of its primary yards and interchange points was at Hagerstown, Maryland, where an Alco RS-3, Alco FAs, and an EMD SD40 are seen on May 13, 1972. Much of WM's line essentially duplicated B&O's and was abandoned after Chessie System absorbed the railroad. *R.R. Richardson, Doug Eisele collection*

Opposite: Richmond, Virginia, is the location of America's only triple railway crossing. Over the years a variety of photos have been posed here, and this was the last time three separate railroads were represented. This one, taken on July 18, 1983, depicts the early CSX era, when the Chessie System and Seaboard System images were still in vogue. From top to bottom, the historic lines are the Chesapeake & Ohio's James River Line, Seaboard Air Line's mainline, and Southern Railway's branchline to West Point, Virginia. *Doug Koontz*

After months of detailed hearings, the Interstate Commerce Commission approved the C&O control of B&O on December 17, 1962. Saunders indicates that this decision was made in the wake of the Cuban Missile Crisis and influenced by a Cold War mentality. At the time, Langdon argued that the financial collapse of the B&O could weaken America's ability to fight a war. What is especially interesting about this round of merger planning was how C&O/B&O was both a reaction to Penn Central and helped pave the way for it.

The Penn Central merger finally occurred in 1968. By all accounts, it was a total disaster. In 1970, PC collapsed in the largest corporate bankruptcy up to that time. The failure of Penn Central and five other eastern railroads made it seem that the railroad industry itself was on the verge of collapse. The federal government was now forced to sort out the mess, and ultimately this resulted in the 1976 creation of Consolidated Rail Corporation (Conrail) from the bankrupt ruins of PC and other northeastern roads in dire straits.

To many observers, Conrail seemed to be that old boogieman: nationalization. In truth, it was different than pure federal ownership and control, although billions of tax dollars and much government planning went into making Conrail a profitable and, ultimately, a privately owned operation. The irony in this exercise was that two decades after it was created to consolidate Eastern rail operations, Conrail was split and sold to the successors of Norfolk & Western and Chesapeake & Ohio. CSX bought the core of the old New York Central, and Norfolk Southern bought the core of the old Pennsy.

Chessie System

C&O/B&O was not a formal merger. Both companies maintained their corporate names. In his July 1989 *TRAINS Magazine* article, Langdon explains that initially B&O enjoyed an influx of leased C&O coal hoppers, which it desperately needed "to relieve a chronic shortage." He also wrote that in 1964 after C&O management assumed control, many of the old B&O people left. Langdon's conclusion does

8295
8295
C&O
8295
Chessie System
SEABOARD
SYSTEM
6719
6719
6143
6143H
SOUTHERN

2101
2101
2101
Chessie STEAM SPECIAL

In the late 1970s, the Chessie System dressed up former Reading Company T-1 2102 to run a series of passenger specials over its lines. On May 13, 1978, a Chessie Steam Special ascends the east slope of Sand Patch and rounds the horseshoe curve at Mance, Pennsylvania, in the driving rain. ***George Kowanski***

not paint C&O management in the best light. He asserts that while C&O control benefited B&O's shareholders, "the takeover was a step backwards" in regards to service in Maryland, and specifically the Port of Baltimore. With C&O control, B&O no longer functioned for the purposes for which it was built, but served C&O's financial interests.

As the C&O/B&O control case was under review by the federal government, C&O bought up Western Maryland stock, 43 percent of which B&O already had owned since the 1920s. As a result of the 1914 Clayton antitrust act, B&O had not been allowed to control WM because the two lines were parallel and competed for the same traffic, so its stock was held in trust. By the mid-1960s, WM's competitive position was less of a concern; C&O/B&O was granted control of WM in February 1967. Over the next decade, WM gradually disappeared into the Chessie System.

In a separate case, the ICC approved C&O's control of America's last interurban electric railway, the Chicago, South Shore & South Bend, in 1966. The line remained in C&O's portfolio until 1985, when it was sold again.

As the Penn Central merger progressed, C&O and N&W entered into serious negotiations to join their respective railroad empires. In 1968, it appeared that C&O/N&W was on its way to ICC approval; however, the crash of Penn Central in 1970 contributed to C&O and N&W's decision to call it off in 1971.

One of C&O's stars was Hays Watkins. He was hired in 1949 and appointed as a vice president in 1964. Richard W. Barsness, in

On December 30, 1985, a Chessie System freight led by B&O GP40-2 rolls though the streets of Lawrenceburg, Indiana. ***Bradley McClelland***

A remanufactured locomotive, designated GP16, leads an eastward Seaboard System freight on the L&N route at Pascagoula, Mississippi, on November 16, 1985. In the 1970s, Seaboard Coast Line, Louisville & Nashville, and affiliated railroads were marketed as the Family Lines. On January 1, 1983, CSX created Seaboard System from the Family Lines railroads. Pascagoula is on the former L&N Mobile to New Orleans mainline and was known as M&NO Sub of the Mobile Division during the L&N days. ***John Leopard***

Railroads in the Age of Regulation, 1900–1980, explains that Watkins was greatly influenced by John Kusik, the man who helped push the C&O/B&O combination. In 1971, Watkins assumed the role of president and chief executive officer of C&O/B&O. Watkins' proactive approach to railroading was in contrast to the industry in general, which was seen as stodgy and declining. In an era when railroads were slow to react to shippers' needs and inflexible toward an evolving market, Watkins set out to improve customer focus. He looked to upgrade his lines' basic product: service.

The familiar Chessie kitten insignia had been a traditional C&O symbol for decades, and the railroad had long been informally known as Chessie. Robert Young's stillborn luxury streamliner was going to be called the *Chessie,* so as the C&O/B&O combination coalesced, it was unofficially known as the Chessie System.

Sometimes a popular nickname is better than a traditional one. In the wake of the dissolution of the proposed C&O/N&W combination, Watkins oversaw the creation of Chessie System Incorporated in February 1973. This was the holding company for C&O, B&O, and Western Maryland. Chessie System Railroads was the new image with an old name. A new locomotive livery that fulfilled the aesthetic ideals of the mid-1970s was adopted in place of the C&O/B&O–era royal blue and yellow. This featured a predominantly bright yellow body, vermillion and blue striping, with a large stylized Chessie kitten as the company logo prominently displayed on the front of each locomotive. Equipment continued to be sub-lettered for each of the constituent railways. Brightly painted Chessie System locomotives were a stark contrast to the somber black of Penn Central. Where PC seemed to represent doom, Chessie presented an image of hope. Watkins was one of the most progressive leaders in the industry. He planned to reform his railroads by reducing redundancy, excess capacity, and make them more competitive with other modes of transportation.

The 1970s were dark times for American railroads, especially in the Northeast. Penn Central's failings had first resulted in the creation of Amtrak in 1971 to relieve all American railroads of their obligation to provide intercity passenger services and retain a skeletal intercity network. Government planners hoped to involve solvent carriers in the creation of Conrail by encouraging healthy roads to purchase all or part of some bankrupt lines. This strategy was to offer competition to the government-sponsored Conrail and alleviate concerns of a total nationalization of the railroad industry. Initially Chessie's Watkins was enthusiastic. According to H. Roger Grant in his book *Erie Lackawanna—Death of an American Railroad, 1938–1992,* Watkins looked to expand the B&O by assuming operation of most of the Erie Lackawanna east of Sterling, Ohio (near Akron), as well as much of the Reading, and Penn Central's route to Charleston, West Virginia. This resulted in a vicious fight within the company, but Watkins prevailed and in June 1975, Chessie System tentatively agreed to the acquisition. The creation of Conrail was on a rigid schedule for April 1, 1976, and as that day approached, Chessie System's acquisition plan unraveled. One stumbling block was the price Chessie would pay for its new routes. Labor issues, however, were a more serious concern. Grant explains, "The gulf between labor and management was probably too wide to bridge." Weeks before Conrail's birth, Chessie backed out, and Delaware & Hudson was recruited to provide competition to Conrail using trackage rights largely over EL and Reading routes that Chessie would have operated.

Among Watkins' successful crusades was pushing for deregulation to help the industry regain its competitive edge. Canada had initiated deregulation in 1967, and this had

As seen from the cab of a southward freight, Seaboard Coast Line SD45 2036 leads northward freight 227 at Collier, Virginia, on the old Atlantic Coast Line mainline. On the SCL, the SD45s with their 20-cylinder 645-E3 engines were known as Clydesdales among the operating crews. ***Doug Riddell***

Sometimes you need a scorecard to unravel the mysteries of modern railroading. On March 19, 1989, a pair of Seaboard System C30-7s lead CSX's daily freight from Detroit to Buffalo, New York, on Conrail's former New York Central at CP437 near the old Buffalo Central Terminal. This CSX freight followed the old Pere Marquette route across Ontario and reached Buffalo via Niagara Falls and Conrail's Niagara Branch. To the right is an eastward Conrail freight heading toward Frontier Yard. *Brian Solomon*

proved very successful. Watkins was a firm supporter of the Staggers Act, which was passed in 1980. This legislation freed the railroads from the shackles of strict government rate regulation and helped reinvigorate the industry.

Seaboard Coast Line

The health of the railroad industry was a hot topic in the late 1950s. In 1958, Congress investigated the matter, but to the disgust of some railroads, it failed to come up with plausible solutions, aid, or a plan. John Smith, Seaboard Air Line's president, and Atlantic Coast Line's W. Thomas Rice reacted by proposing a merger. This was an unusual and very significant move because up until that time, most merger schemes either paired weak lines with strong ones, or looked to coordinate weak parallel railroads. ACL and SAL were well-run lines that had shown tidy profits for more than a decade and were virtually parallel everywhere they went, but ACL and SAL faced disturbing trends. Both lines had robust and growing traffic, but profits were not growing proportionally. They watched as highway and airline competition eroded their most lucrative traffic. A staple of their north-south routes was the perishable business—traffic that they had practically invented—and "snowbird" passenger traffic from the Northeast to Florida. By 1958, the real competition to the railroads was from the highways and airlines, not from each other.

In 1960, ACL and SAL enthusiastically agreed on a merger. Interstate Commerce

In October 1988, CSX's daily Buffalo-Detroit freight crosses Suspension Bridge over the Niagara Gorge, which serves as the border between the United States and Canada. This train followed a Pere Marquette route. Today, CSX uses the former New York Central mainline through Buffalo and no longer operates on the PM route across Ontario. *Brian Solomon*

Commission hearings began in 1961, about the same time as the C&O/B&O hearings. There was loud opposition from labor, shippers who feared the loss of competition, the Justice Department, and notably from Southern Railway and Illinois Central who protested because of ACL's involvement with Louisville & Nashville and related properties. While L&N was not involved in ACL/SAL merger discussions, the other railroads could imagine where this merger might lead.

Despite objections, ICC approved ACL/SAL in December 1963. The merger was delayed because of continuing legal activity aimed at prying L&N away from ACL. These attempts failed and the merger was consummated on July 1, 1967—almost nine years after it was first suggested. Rice was named president and chief executive officer. In *TRAINS Magazine*, David P. Morgan notes the significance of ICC's decision: "This was the first instance in modern merger history of two comfortably solvent and parallel major railroads seeking unification." Morgan went on to echo the implication of the Commission's ground-breaking decision, "Rails no longer dominate transportation." Smith and Rice had taken a gamble when they suggested they join forces, and they won.

The Seaboard Coast Line blended the names of its predecessors. It started with 9,624 route miles. From the beginning, the company looked to downgrade and abandon redundant lines. The largely directional double-track ACL mainline was preferred over the SAL single-track main with its difficult sawtooth profile. A variety of Seaboard's secondary routes were also ripe for trimming.

A 1967 SCL advertisement in *TRAINS Magazine* that proclaimed the new railroad explained:

"Why have we merged? For very practical reasons. To cut costs. To become more diversified and efficient. In short, to enable ourselves to offer shippers and passengers a broader range of services and equipment; faster, more flexible schedules; greater economies in transportation."

Not everyone was impressed with SCL. In *Merging Lines,* Saunders draws a dim conclusion of SCL. "The new company should have been a success. It had good management and plenty of cash to make the necessary physical changes, and traffic volumes continued to grow. But it was not a success. It was not a catastrophe, either, but shippers

Three nearly new Seaboard System SD50s lead a coal train near Independence, Kentucky. In 1985, prior to CSX phasing out both Chessie System and Seaboard System images in favor of the corporate CSXT image, the company ordered SD50s from General Motors' Electro-Motive Division. These were painted for both railroads but occupied a common number block. ***Bradley McClelland***

Left: Louisville & Nashville operated an extensive network of coal-gathering lines in eastern Kentucky. Coal was marshaled to yards at centralized points and assembled into larger trains. L&N purchased large numbers of Alco diesels that were used into the 1980s. On May 7, 1980, L&N C-420 1377 works with a General Electric U25B at the yard in Loyall, Kentucky. *George S. Pitarys*

Below: A General Electric–built DASH 8-40C leads a northward loaded GALX coal train on the former Louisville & Nashville Rockhouse Creek Branch, now CSX's EK Subdivision near Colson, Kentucky, on December 28, 1994. This train was loaded on the former C&O E&BV branch at the Bates branch tipple and is destined to the electric utility Stilesboro plant at Cartersville, Georgia. *William M. Beecher, Jr.*

Running southward on the former Monon, CSX Q642 led by a pair of DASH 8-40CWs has just passed through Shelby, Indiana, and nears the crossroads of Monon Avenue and 205th Street at the far southeastern end of suburban Chicago on June 30, 2001. *Eric Powell*

throughout Florida were screaming before long. . . ."

Less than two years after the SCL merger, SCL absorbed the Piedmont Northern, which operated lines in North and South Carolina.

Louisville & Nashville Reaches Chicago

Chicago & Eastern Illinois was a medium-sized line that was a little over 900 miles long with a route map that resembled an inverted tree; Chicago sat at the base of the trunk with primary branches to St. Louis, southern Illinois gateways at Thebes and Joppa, and an Indiana gateway at Evansville. In the 1920s it enjoyed robust coal traffic from southern Illinois, but this traffic declined during the Great Depression. In more recent years, the railroad had served as a bridgeline for Missouri Pacific and Louisville & Nashville and forwarded freight and passenger traffic to Chicago. During the 1960s, C&EI and L&N jointly operated an intermodal run from Chicago to Nashville and Atlanta.

C&EI discussed a merger with Missouri Pacific in 1960, but when MoPac failed to make an immediate offer, it looked to L&N. This led to both L&N and MoPac vying for control. Ultimately, the two railroads agreed to divide C&EI. The ICC approved MoPac's purchase of C&EI in February 1967, which included the provision that it sell L&N the eastern route from Evansville to Danville and Woodland Junction, Illinois, with trackage rights to Chicago. The ICC approved the details of L&N's C&EI purchase in October 1968, and L&N finally introduced through traffic to Chicago in 1969. In addition to the new route, L&N also acquired a share of C&EI equipment, including 48 locomotives and approximately 1,500 freight cars. L&N used Belt Railway of Chicago in the Chicago terminal. This acquisition was a crucial route for L&N, and it still remains important to CSX.

L&N's C&EI acquisition caused the Monon line to squawk. Like C&EI, Monon forwarded L&N traffic to Chicago. So while L&N was negotiating with MoPac, it simultaneously moved to acquire Monon. Monon operated approximately 540 route miles,

The CSX network inherited a variety of duplicative routes, and some have been pruned from the map. While a portion of the old Monon remains integral to CSX, other segments have been abandoned. Although predecessor Louisville & Nashville used both of its north-south Indiana routes, CSX downgraded the former Monon Railroad mainline in 1993 in favor of its ex-C&EI route following a washout that effectively severed the line. The section to go was the 15-mile segment between Cloverdale and Gosport, and the abandonment was effective March 1994. One year later, the aftermath of the scrappers' work can be seen at the Indiana Southern Railroad (former Pennsylvania Railroad) crossing at Gosport. *Scott Muskopf*

In a scene somewhat reminiscent to the opening of the movie *Hoosiers*, CSX grain train G620 skirts barren, frigid cornfields north of Ladoga, Indiana, seconds before sunset, at 5:18 p.m. on December 27, 2002. CSX SD50 8549 and DASH 8-40C 7562 lead 65 grain loads south across the jointed rail that was once the Fourth, or Middle Subdivision, of the Monon Railroad's Chicago–Louisville mainline. This train will take the connection at Greencastle that was built in 1992, and utilize CSX's former Big Four Indianapolis–St. Louis mainline as far as Terre Haute, where it will roll onto CSX's former Chicago & Eastern Illinois mainline toward Evansville, Indiana, and points south. *Eric Powell*

which formed a gigantic "X" within Indiana. It reached both Louisville and Chicago via trackage rights. The crossing of its primary Indianapolis–Chicago and Louisville–Michigan City lines was the village of Monon, Indiana, from which the railroad took its trade name. In the steam era, Monon's full name had been Chicago, Indianapolis & Louisville Railway. The merger was consummated on August 1, 1971. Although it wasn't as important as the C&EI route, Monon's 325-mile line between Louisville and Chicago provided L&N with an alternate Chicago connection and allowed for more direct routing for traffic moving on the eastern portion of the railroad, while giving L&N access to Indianapolis.

Another L&N acquisition occurred in 1969 when it bought the Nashville and Crossville portion of the defunct Tennessee Central, which had been divided three ways, and Southern Railway and Illinois Central bought the other portions.

Family Lines

Seaboard Coast Line Industries Incorporated was formed in 1969 as a parent to the Seaboard Coast Line Railroad Company. This

Left: In 1977, at Bryan Park, Richmond, Virginia, Family Lines office car No. 308 is coupled with Richmond, Fredericksburg & Potomac car *One* and awaits the arrival of company officials, including W. T. Rice. *Doug Riddell*

Below: Four-motor GEs lead a northbound freight at Chaska, Tennessee, on CSX's Corbin Division on July 20, 1990. This train operating is en route from Atlanta to Cincinnati on the former L&N mainline crossing the mountains of Tennessee. Chaska is a helper base where trains pick up extra locomotives for assistance over the grade to the south. *Doug Koontz*

allowed the company to diversify its business. At that time, Seaboard Coast Line owned one-third stock in L&N, but it began to increase its holdings. SCL and L&N had equal holdings in the Clinchfield and Georgia Railroads. By the end of 1971, SCL Industries had acquired 98 percent of L&N stock. In 1972, SCL Industries exercised its influence over L&N when the companies' executives played a game of high-level musical chairs. Author Maury Klein explained that SCL Railroad's president Prime F. Osborn III gave up that position for the presidency of L&N, while L&N's president William Kendall moved to become the vice-chairman of SCL Industries. W. Thomas Rice remained in the top position.

Reflecting these boardroom maneuverings and the tightening of long-standing relationships, in 1972 SCL decided to jointly market SCL, L&N, Clinchfield, and the Georgia Railroads as the "Family Lines." This was not a merger, but rather a public face that reflected the family-like affiliation of SCL Industries' railroads. Under Family Lines, the railroads retained their corporate identities, and while locomotives and equipment were painted with the new Family Lines livery—gray with yellow and red stripes—sub-lettering indicated equipment ownership. The source of the paychecks remained the same.

CSX Is Born

Railroad consolidation continued during the 1970s. In the mid-1970s, Southern Pacific bought 10 percent of SCL Industries as a prelude to a possible merger. SCL had its own ideas about a merger and turned SP down. On November 14, 1978, the CSX Corporation was chartered in Virginia as a holding company for the proposed merger of SCL Industries and Chessie System. Corporate headquarters was located at Richmond, Virginia, which was the headquarters of SCL Industries and an important administrative center on Chessie's C&O. Jacksonville, Florida, remained as SCL Railroad's headquarters. CSX symbolically represented the joining of the two transportation giants—"C" for Chessie, "S" for Seaboard, and "X" for multiplied; it is neither an abbreviation nor an acronym.

On January 18, 1979, Chessie System and SCL Industries sought approval from the ICC for merger of the two railroad holding companies. Chessie System was the seventh largest American railroad company, while SCL Industries was fifth. The proposed CSX combination spurred reaction from the region's two other giants, Norfolk & Western and Southern Railway, and on April 5, 1979, these railroads announced that they were considering a merger. Meanwhile, Southern Railway opposed the CSX merger. In July 1980, Chessie and Seaboard placated Southern by easing its operations in the proposed Norfolk Southern merger in exchange for Southern dropping its opposition to CSX.

The ICC approved this decision, and on November 1, 1980, the CSX Corporation holding company was officially formed as a merger of Seaboard Coast Line Industries with Chessie System. Under the CSX umbrella, there were now approximately 28,000 route miles operating in 20 states and two Canadian provinces. It was the largest railroad in the United States. SCL's Prime F. Osborn became CSX chairman, while Chessie's Hays T. Watkins was named president, and both men were co-chief executive officers. For the time being, Chessie System and SCL railroads retained independent identities, and operations remained largely unchanged. Locomotives and equipment were still painted and lettered for the individual lines and not for CSX. Locomotives continued to operate on their home systems. Norfolk & Western and Southern merged, forming Norfolk Southern two years after the formation of CSX.

Seaboard System

In preparation for the eventual merger of the SCL Industries railroads with Chessie Systems, an internal consolidation took place in

December 1982 when the Seaboard Coast Line Railroad was merged with L&N. On January 1, 1983, the SCL railroads became known as the Seaboard System Railroad, which was a move that consummated the complex relationship that had existed under the Family Lines. Gone were the historic L&N, Clinchfield, and Georgia Railroad names. Seaboard System embraced a new image, but it was cosmetically similar to Family Lines. The new livery was much like Family Lines', but streamlined and cleaner. Locomotives were painted gray with a stylized "SS" logo in red and yellow. When it was introduced, the Seaboard System operated a 15,408-mile network. It was one of the shortest-lived major railroads in American history and lasted just three and one-half years.

CSX Goes Multimodal

The formation of CSX coincided with the passage of the Staggers Act, the legislation Hays Watkins had championed that deregulated American railroads. According to Richard W. Barsness, Watkins hoped to make CSX more responsive to the transportation market and moved to expand companies' operations into multimodal transportation. Watkins said, "We are no longer just railroads, but total distribution systems. . . . Railroads can—and are—getting into related lines of business like trucking, warehousing, and bulk distribution." His "One Stop Shipping" philosophy dominated CSX's further expansion over the next two decades. To expand its trailer on flatcar (TOFC) business, CSX formed the Chessie Motor Express in 1981. This

A pair of Seaboard System F units lead a director's special at Rocky Mount, North Carolina, in February 1985. No. 118 was Clinchfield's sole FP7 and originally carried the number 200. In the CSX era, these former Clinchfield Fs were based in Waycross, Georgia. ***Doug Riddell***

trucking service was designed to deliver truck trailers from shippers to 47 intermodal terminals across the CSX system.

Following Osborn's retirement in 1982, Watkins became CSX chairman. Watkins continued multimodal acquisitions. In 1983, he moved to purchase the Texas Gas Resource Corporation, which operated 6,000 miles of pipelines and America's foremost barge common carrier called American Commercial Lines. This purchase was a significant test case that fueled significant opposition outside the industry. As the ICC prepared to review the case in February 1984, the *Washington Post* quoted Joe Farrell, president of the American Waterways Operators Inc., "This is the landmark transportation case of the century." He was opposed to the merger, which he felt would eliminate competition. By contrast, Watkins said, "In my opinion, it is time to stop talking of rail or truck or barge or pipeline transportation in isolation and to start talking about transportation." Despite long-standing objections and provisions that stemmed from the 1912 Panama Canal Act that prohibited a railroad from owning a water carrier it competed against, the ICC approved the CSX Corporation merger with American Commercial Lines in July 1984. The barge company was CSX's primary interest in the acquisition of Texas Gas Transmission, and in 1988, CSX divested the company and its 6,000-mile pipeline but retained the barge operation.

In 1986, CSX Corporation purchased the American-owned international shipping company Sea-Land. Based in Menlo Park, New Jersey, Sea-Land was the largest American containership company. It had a fleet of 57 seagoing container ships and served 76 ports in 64 countries. A year earlier, Sea-Land was one of the first companies involved in transcontinental land-bridge container service using newly developed double-stack container trains. Noteworthy was double-stack service to the New York metro area that bypassed

During the summer of 1988, an A-B configuration of former Clinchfield F units leads CSX's Southbound RoadRailer train as it exits the tunnel at Brush Creek, Kentucky, on CSX's Corbin Division. The short-lived train transported auto parts between Detroit, Michigan, and Atlanta, Georgia, and was often assigned CSX's F units, which were more typically reserved for business trains. *Doug Koontz*

Conrail by using a CSX (B&O)–Delaware & Hudson–New York, Susquehanna & Western route. The July 21, 1986, *Traffic World* quoted Watkins, "We have recognized the need to become a truly intermodal company. We are proud of the fact that with our rail, truck, barge, and pipeline companies we're the first *domestic* intermodal company. Recognizing the increasing *international* nature of business, we hope to become the first international transportation company."

The U.S. Department of Transportation supported CSX's Sea-Land acquisition, and stated in the October 20, 1986, *Traffic World,* " . . .The public will benefit from new competitive service and enhanced coordination in service and reductions in costs that will result from common ownership."

Fight for Conrail: Round One

In its first four years, Conrail soaked up billions of tax dollars, but continued to suffer from lackluster performance which led to fears that it would become a perpetual drain on government resources. New leadership, aided by the passage of the Staggers Act, helped Conrail turn the corner. On January 1, 1981, former Southern Railway Chairman L. Stanley Crane became Conrail's chairman and chief executive. One of the most respected executives in the industry, Crane transformed Conrail into a lean, profitable railroad. Crane hacked away at Conrail's route map and trimmed numerous branches, as well as some redundant mainlines from the system. He cut the ranks of labor. He extricated Conrail from the commuter rail business. On the political front, Crane fought to allow the railroad to

116
CSX
116

In 1986, CSX Transportation began to replace the names of CSX's component railroads. *Brian Solomon*

CSX Transportation logo as printed on the side of a business car. *Brian Solomon*

continue as Conrail. At the time, the Reagan Administration wanted to liquidate the massive railroad and sell its lines to the highest bidders. Crane convinced the government to hold off selling Conrail until he could get the railroad back in the black.

Under Crane, Conrail earned its first and largest profits. In 1983, the Reagan Administration renewed action to sell Conrail. They hoped to auction it off to another profitable carrier, preferably one with sufficiently deep pockets to withstand the next economic downturn. Initially, both of the newly formed eastern giants, Norfolk Southern and CSX, were interested. Ultimately, the government received 18 bids for Conrail, and while NS bid, CSX did not. The NS bid was deemed the most desirable, and during 1985 and early 1986, the government's plans to sell Conrail to NS moved forward. There was tremendous opposition. Consider CSX's Watkins' testimony to Congress:

"We made a careful study of a possible purchase by CSX and concluded there would be a great benefit to CSX. After all, Conrail is a very significant customer and competitor of CSX, and buying Conrail would eliminate that competition and forever capture the traffic for CSX, which now flows from Conrail. We also concluded that very much of the same analysis would apply to Norfolk Southern. It only pays to be a monopolist if you can get away with it. Our study convinced us that a CSX or Norfolk Southern proposal to buy Conrail would not survive any rational scrutiny under the antitrust concepts that have governed every railroad merger in this country."

Faced with losing as much as $400 million from a Conrail/NS merger, Watkins threatened to dump the B&O rather than attempt to compete with the merged company.

Crane, who had helped conceive Norfolk Southern when he was Southern's chairman, also opposed the NS/Conrail combination. Instead he proposed a sale to the public that would allow Conrail to remain independent. The opposition won out, and the sale to NS was scuttled. In August 1986, NS withdrew its bid, and on March 26, 1987, a few days shy of Conrail's 11th birthday, the federal government's share in Conrail was sold as initial public offering on the New York Stock Exchange. A decade later, Conrail was a hot topic.

Four CSX SD40-2s are down on their hands and knees in run-8 and making a thunderous noise as this train approaches Big Stone Gap, Virginia, in 1989. Regular attendees at the Robinette Baptist Chapel may not appreciate the thrill of CSX action on a Sunday morning, but on this weekday afternoon it seems just right. This train operated by trackage rights on Norfolk Southern track in southwestern Virginia. This arrangement resulted from Norfolk Southern and CSX trading equal trackage rights between Big Stone Gap, Virginia, and Frisco, Tennessee, to help shorten the routes for coal trains of both railroads. *Doug Koontz*

CSX Transportation

The "CSX" name, which had been coined in 1978 as the tentative name for the holding company to merge Seaboard Coast Line and Chessie System, finally emerged as the railroad name in 1986. In *TRAINS Magazine*, David P. Morgan wrote, "CSX was supposed to be just a temporary moniker until public relations could come up with a name to replace the initials, but it caught on, then blossomed. . . ."

The creation of CSX Transportation was part of a larger restructuring of CSX Corporation when four primary subsidiaries were established, including CSX Energy, CSX Property, and CSX Technology. CSX Transportation was created in 1986 and the first locomotives emerged in a demonstration CSXT livery in April. On July 1, Seaboard System was the first of CSX Corporation's component railroads to be folded into CSXT. In preparation for Chessie System to be consolidated into CSXT, the Baltimore & Ohio was officially merged with C&O on April 30, 1987. Functionally, Baltimore & Ohio had been part of C&O for two decades. In the January 1991 issue of *TRAINS Magazine*,

CSX R123 southbound intermodal freight led by B36-7 5897 passes beneath a steam-age relic in Sullivan, Indiana, on the morning of February 3, 1991. This coaling tower was built by the Chicago & Eastern Illinois Railroad, whose Chicago–Evansville, Indiana, mainline was acquired by the L&N in 1969. This route has become a key CSX artery between Chicago and the Southeast. *Scott Muskopf*

Herbert H. Harwood Jr. explained that Chessie System and CSX had maintained B&O's separate identity as a result of "quirks in its debt structure and its Maryland tax exemption." Then on September 2, 1987, C&O was merged into CSXT. It was the last of the original component railroads to lose its identity. The delay of melding C&O into CSXT was a result of the need to satisfy the legal requirements of its Canadian operations.

The CSXT blanket effectively covered the company's vast railroad operations that had been traditionally operated by well-known historic railroads. The loss of these railroads' identity caused considerable concern. To make things difficult for the spin doctors following the creation of CSXT was the fact that when CSX was created, it asserted that component railroads' identities would be maintained. In the March 1981 issue of *TRAINS Magazine*, Milton B. Dolinger, CSX's director of public relations, had been quoted (from a letter to the editor in the *Tulsa Tribune*), "You will never see 'CSX' on the side of a boxcar. We do indeed, intend to continue the identity of Chessie and its components, C&O, B&O, and Western Maryland. Family Lines continue to preserve the L&N, the SCL, and the Clinchfield. . . ." Five years later, with a parenthetic eyebrow raised, Morgan highlighted the incongruity of this statement on the announcement of the creation of CSX Transportation, which prompted a response and clarification from Dolinger. "What I said five years ago was our official position at that time. And, actually, when I said, 'you will never see 'CSX' on the side of a boxcar' it was a correct statement then and remains a correct one today. 'CSX,' by itself, is 'CSX Corporation.' That is a holding company, and you will not see it on equipment. 'CSX Transportation' is the new name for the combined Chessie and

Seaboard railroads, and that's the name you will see on equipment."

The scheme of reporting marks on equipment used by North American railroads used "X" to indicate privately owned railroad cars, and thus "CSXT" was needed to fulfill the requirements of this reporting scheme. While the first CSX-painted locomotives had "CSX Transportation" boldly painted on their sides, by the end of 1986, "Transportation" had been dropped.

(Incidentally, since this book is primarily concerned with CSX's railroad history and operations, "CSX" is used to describe the railroad. Further indicators that distinguish internal corporate structure and restructuring are used herein only when necessary to maintain clarity.)

Changes at the Top

Hays Watkins, who had led Chessie System, engineered the creation of CSX, and was a mover in the rejuvenation of eastern railroading, retired as CSX's chairman in February 1991. John Snow assumed the top position. Snow, who had been an executive with CSX and its predecessors since 1977, had served as the company's president and chief operating officer since 1988. Snow initially continued to implement Watkins' "one-stop shopping" approach until he realized the flaw in this philosophy. In the last years of Snow's

West of Meyersdale, Pennsylvania, a westward CSX freight plies the rails of the old B&O at sunset on October 22, 1992. The Salisbury Viaduct, seen in the distance, is on the old Western Maryland–Connellsville extension—a route built in 1928 at great cost to give the line through connections to the West but abandoned in the 1970s after WM became part of Chessie System. *Brian Solomon*

Among CSX's mid-1980s mainline abandonment was the severing of St. Louis mainline across central West Virginia, west of Clarksburg. This busy line once hosted numerous heavy freights and popular passenger trains such as the *National Limited.* The irony of this abandonment is that in the early 1960s, B&O improved the clearances on the line with aid from West Virginia. It would have made an ideal route for double-stack intermodal trains, which were becoming popular at the time of the line's closure. *Brian Solomon*

administration, he refocused CSXT's business on railroading and had his eyes on Conrail as a means for expansion.

RF&P Comes into the Fold

In February 1990, CSX merged the Richmond, Fredericksburg & Potomac into its network. The RF&P was a 113-mile line that ran from Alexandria, Virginia, to Richmond, and was a strategic route for CSX that neatly connected former B&O routes with those of the Seaboard and C&O. According to *TRAINS Magazine*, by 1989 more than 80 percent of RF&P's traffic was overhead business, and the vast majority bridged between CSX lines. Traditionally, RF&P's six principal connections—B&O, C&O, SAL, ACL, PRR, and Southern Railway—controlled the line through the Richmond–Washington Corporation, which held three-fourths of RF&P voting stock. The collapse of Penn Central ended PRR's control, and by 1990, CSX held roughly 80 percent of Richmond–Washington Corp. and 36 percent of RF&P stock.

CSX's plans did not proceed as smoothly as hoped. The Commonwealth of Virginia was RF&P's other owner, which held a portion of RF&P's voting stock that was not owned by the Richmond–Washington Corp. and opposed the terms of CSX's proposed merger

In 1991, CSX absorbed the Richmond, Fredericksburg & Potomac, a double-track raceway between Washington, D.C., and Richmond. In December 1972, a quartet of RF&P GP40s lead southward freight No. 175 at Elletts, near Ashland, Virginia. Today this route is clogged with freight and passenger traffic. *Jeremy F. Plant*

with RF&P. One point of issue between CSX and the Commonwealth was the fate of RF&P's sprawling Potomac Yards not far from the Pentagon and National Airport, across the river from Washington, D.C. By this time, these yards were RF&P's greatest single asset and were worth much more as commercial property than a classification yard.

Finally after a year and a half of negotiations, CSX and Virginia (via the Virginia Retirement System) jointly bought RF&P on October 10, 1991. Initially, RF&P trains didn't look much different than they had under independent operation. This was primarily a function of the railroad's cab-signal system that required specialized equipment on lead locomotives. The sale of RF&P effectively sealed the fate of Potomac Yard, which was gradually phased out during the mid-1990s.

Pittsburgh & Lake Erie

In 1934 under Daniel Willard, Baltimore & Ohio had arranged for trackage rights over a 61-mile-long section of Pittsburgh & Lake Erie in the Pittsburgh area between McKeesport and New Castle Junction (near West Pittsburgh, Pennsylvania). This gave B&O passenger trains better access to downtown Pittsburgh and provided a shorter, low-grade route for B&O freight so trains could avoid B&O's steeply graded Pittsburgh & Western line.

Under New York Central control, Pittsburgh & Lake Erie had retained considerable independence. It had its own management and maintained its own locomotives and cars at its McKees Rocks Shops. The P&LE was not included in Conrail and remained a private line that was busy and relatively profitable throughout the 1970s. It thrived

Above: The sun sets on Conrail. In May 1999, just two days before Conrail operations were officially split between CSX and Norfolk Southern, an eastward multilevel train catches the glint of the setting sun as it rolls along the Mohawk River at Guy Park, west of Amsterdam, New York. Today this section of the former New York Central Water Level Route is a busy CSX freight corridor. *Brian Solomon*

Right: CSX put its mark on the venerable Goodman Street Yard tower in Rochester, New York. On January 25, 2004, a blanket of snow covers Goodman Street Yard as locomotives idle in the distance. In the mid-1990s, Conrail closed the Atlantic Avenue diesel house and serviced engines at the other end of the yard, adjacent to the yard tower. Until 1986, when it sold the old Buffalo, Rochester & Pittsburgh route of the B&O, CSX had been just a minor player in Rochester, New York. With the acquisition of this Conrail route in 1999, CSX became the dominant railroad in the Rochester area. *Otto M. Vondrak*

Part of the terms of the Conrail split allowed both CSX and Norfolk Southern equal access to key terminal areas, notably those in New Jersey, which were administered as Conrail Shared Assets. On September 24, 2004, a CSX local works beneath the wire on the Northeast Corridor, the former Pennsylvania Railroad New York to Philadelphia mainline. *Patrick Yough*

serving coal and steel industries in the Mahoning, Monongahela, and Ohio River Valleys. When the U.S. steel industry collapsed in the early 1980s due to foreign competition, so did P&LE's profits. Conrail's improved financial condition made things worse for P&LE. By the mid-1980s, P&LE was essentially operating a single through freight daily, and the majority of traffic on its lines was B&O's and accounted for up to 20 through freights daily.

The railroad was in a tailspin. The loss of once-lucrative traffic resulted in P&LE cutting most of its employment. In September 1986, the situation had reached a low point and P&LE's unions called a strike over the takeover by the West Pullman Transportation Corporation. The P&LE reacted by single-tracking its line and placing severe speed restrictions over most of the route. Beginning in October, CSX was forced to detour traffic away from P&LE and use its own P&W route instead. The P&W's sinuous, heavily grade line was ill-suited to accommodate modern traffic flows. CSX assigned helpers to assist heavy westward trains. The detours only lasted a few weeks, but CSX recognized that using P&LE's rails could not be taken for granted.

In 1988, CSX tried to organize a joint purchase of P&LE with the latter's employees, but failed to come to a mutually suitable agreement with P&LE's unions. The railroad languished for a few more years. In 1991, CSX purchased the crucial 61-mile segment from P&LE and arranged to lease back the line to P&LE. Then in September 1992, CSX further secured its operation over P&LE with the purchase of significant P&LE assets by its new Three Rivers Railway subsidiary. This transaction included P&LE's mainline from Brownsville to McKeesport, Pennsylvania, and from New Castle Junction, Pennsylvania,

CSX control brought a variety of changes to former Conrail properties. A CSX B36-7 leads a 91-car local freight over the old Boston & Albany route at North Wilbraham, Massachusetts, in May 2002. When CSX assumed operations of this former Conrail route, it assigned CSX-painted GP40-2s and B36-7s to local freights that had previously been assigned Conrail B23-7s and GP15-1s. ***Brian Solomon***

to Youngstown, Ohio, plus trackage rights over Conrail to Ashtabula, Ohio. CSX was not interested in remaining P&LE lines, subsidiaries, and assets, which were sold separately by P&LE's parent company.

Fight for Conrail: Round Two

Following a decade of relatively few major changes to the North American rail map, American railroads entered a tumultuous period in 1994 when a new series of massive mergers were proposed. This began with the June 1994 announcement of the Burlington Northern and Santa Fe merger.

In the wake of BNSF, Norfolk Southern renewed its plans for a Conrail merger, but it was shot down in September 1994 when Conrail announced that it was not for sale. Instead, Conrail hoped to further pare down its network. Conrail management also reviewed a variety of options for market expansion, and the most promising bid was for Southern Pacific's Cotton Belt subsidiary in light of Union Pacific's planned purchase of SP. Conrail's bid was unsuccessful and opened it up to renewed merger efforts in the East.

Above: A little more than a month before the end of Conrail operations, train SECS crosses the Upper Bay Bridge at Newark, New Jersey. More has changed than just the railroad since the end of Conrail. *Tim Doherty*

Left: CSX employee, Ryan "Kris" Krengel walks along the running boards of a GP38-2 at South Anderson Yard in Anderson, Indiana, on August 29, 2004. Anderson is located along the former Conrail Big Four mainline (also known as the Bee Line) between Crestline, Ohio, and Indianapolis. *Pete Ruesch*

In a September 20, 1995, *Washington Post* article by transportation specialist Don Phillips, CSX Chairman John Snow said he thought it was inevitable that eastern railroads would merge to form two giant systems. But he said it would be "unthinkable" for Conrail to be solely controlled by NS and suggested a split of the property would be necessary. This was akin to the division of the C&EI 30 years earlier, but on a vaster scale. Snow said, "We'd be satisfied with nothing less than a major division [of Conrail]."

At the time of Snow's discussion, Conrail publicly maintained a desire to remain independent, yet it continued discussions with NS. Hoping to resist NS offers, Conrail's Chairman David LeVan turned to CSX in September 1996. Many in the industry were surprised when CSX and Conrail announced on October 14, 1996, that CSX would purchase Conrail with a stock and cash offer. Norfolk Southern responded almost immediately with a hostile counteroffer. Don Phillips quoted one NS executive as saying, "John [Snow] thought we'd be a bunch of timid southern gentlemen."

Norfolk Southern's counteroffer resulted in a costly bidding war that lasted until January 1997. CSX and NS decided to divide Conrail before seeking merger approval from the federal Surface Transportation Board (STB), the replacement for the former Interstate Commerce Commission, which now maintains federal antitrust oversight for

Above and opposite: **On September 30, 2004, CSX top officials made an inspection of the Boston Line, the former Boston & Albany Railroad, with the company office car train. At the old station location of Middlefield, Massachusetts, the office cars pass intermodal train Q119 slugging it out on the tough climb over the Berkshires with a General Electric 500 series AC4400CW and a General Motors SD70MAC in the lead. Leading the inspection train are two former Amtrak F40PHs. Bringing up the rear of the office car train is the former Conrail Theater Car, which was rebuilt from an old Canadian National diner. Conrail officers made regular use of the railroad's business train, but CSX trips were less frequent.** ***Brian Solomon***

transport. However, since the terms of CSX's original Conrail purchase offer barred it from splitting the railroad with NS, Conrail shareholders rejected CSX's original bid on January 17, 1997. In June 1997, CSX and NS filed their Conrail plan with the STB; CSX would acquire 43 percent of Conrail routes that primarily consisted of former New York Central lines from New York and New England to as far west as Cleveland; Conrail's St. Louis Line; the western end of the Fort Wayne Line; the Toledo–Columbus route; and a route between Philadelphia, Pennsylvania, and Newark, New Jersey, comprised of former Reading and Lehigh Valley lines. Norfolk Southern's share included most remaining former Pennsy lines, plus related Lehigh Valley and Reading routes, the former Erie Railroad Southern Tier, and Conrail's highly prized former NYC line west of Cleveland to Chicago. The dissection of routes through Cleveland was an especially tricky business, but the most complex arrangement was the creation of the Conrail Shared Assets Organization to jointly operate terminal lines in New Jersey, Philadelphia, and

On July 10, 2004, an SD70MAC leads an intermodal train northward along the Hudson River near Ft. Montgomery on CSX's River Line—the former New York Central West Shore route inherited from Conrail in 1999. The famous Bear Mountain Bridge looms in the distance. *Brian Solomon*

Detroit. In essence, the Shared Assets provided an arrangement for both CSX and NS to reach important customers without the need for complex and controversial trackage rights.

The STB gave oral approval for the Conrail split on June 8, 1998. Formal approval was given on July 23, 1998, and contained the board's conditions and concessions granted to other carriers. Beginning on August 22, 1998, NS and CSX had the power to control operations on Conrail. While the details of the split were worked out, Conrail continued to function as a separate railroad until June 1, 1999. After that, Conrail existed as a stock company solely owned by CSX and NS. Conrail leased assets, including locomotives and freight cars, to CSX under the "NYC" designation, and to NS under the "PRR" designation to reflect the heritage of the respective parts of Conrail acquired by the two lines.

The Conrail acquisition greatly expanded CSX's operations, and today CSX is the largest railroad in the eastern United States. Winning Conrail, however, was less of a battle than digesting it. Both NS and CSX made national news as a result of post-merger traffic disruptions. Integrating massive and complex railroad operations had taxed CSX's resources. Unlike difficulties in earlier years resulting from declining traffic, CSX suffered from burgeoning traffic and its insufficient capacity to accommodate the traffic. Its problems stemmed from years of infrastructure pruning that eliminated excess capacity and reduced flexibility. Today when traffic surges, there often is no extra capacity to handle it. Sorting out a bottleneck at one spot just moves the congestion down the line. Yards and terminals are among CSX's worst bottlenecks. During the third quarter of 1999, CSX's largest yards reported car dwell times in excess of 30 hours. The February 2001 issue of *TRAINS Magazine* reported that during the height of the post-Conrail meltdown in November 1999, CSX's Cumberland Yard reported car dwell times of 56 hours. By September 2000, this had been reduced to 19.4 hours. Since those chaotic times, the system has been made more fluid, although some serious bottlenecks, such as in Richmond, Virginia, remain.

Executive Elevation

John Snow left his position as CSX's CEO in early 2003 to take the political appointment as the U.S. secretary of the treasury. In the March 2003 issue of *TRAINS Magazine*, Don Phillips explained that under Snow's tenure, CSX had retrenched from Watkins' one-stop-shopping approach. "Snow tried to make the conglomerate work, but eventually saw the wisdom of selling Sea-Land and most of [American Commercial Barge Lines] to concentrate on the railroad business. Selling those units also helped shed some of the debt load from Snow's major CSX legacy, the division of Conrail with Norfolk Southern." Michael Ward, president of CSX Transportation since 2000, was promoted to replace Snow. Ward started his railroad career in 1977 as a research analyst with Chessie System and held a variety of executive positions with CSX over the years.

Trimming CSX's Map

Since Seaboard Coast Line was first proposed in the 1950s, the rationalization of redundant lines was seen as a means to obtain savings and cut costs. Planners always hope to focus

A portion of the old Atlantic Coast Line mainline near the Virginia–North Carolina state line retains its traditional double track. A former Conrail SD60M leads a southward freight and is about to enter North Carolina on February 20, 2004. *Brian Solomon*

CSX
4741
4741

A new SD70MAC grinds upgrade near milepost 131 west of Middlefield, Massachusetts, on the old Boston & Albany mainline. The ascent of Washington Hill has been challenging railroad operations for more than 160 years. CSX is just the latest company to move trains over this tough piece of mountain railroad. *Brian Solomon*

through traffic on fewer mainlines, while cutting unprofitable and marginally profitable lines. However, few mainlines were cut until the 1980s. Stanley Crane had shown the way with his ruthless cutting of Conrail's duplicative lines. Crane cut more than just Conrail branches and chopped away at redundant mainlines. Among his casualties was most of the former Pennsylvania Railroad Panhandle, which he shut down overnight in 1981.

The old B&O was a prime target for CSX's rationalization efforts. Despite the Staggers Act of 1980s, in the first half of the decade, railroaders still treated the industry as if it were declining. Watkins, a C&O man, had little nostalgia for this historic property. Many B&O lines had been built for a level of traffic that had vanished by the 1980s. One example was the Parkersburg Branch, B&O's former mainline between Clarksburg and Parkersburg. This single-track line was once a major bottleneck that had warranted CTC to increase capacity, but by the mid-1980s, it hosted just a daily pair of intermodal trains and one or two pairs of merchandise trains—four to six through trains every 24 hours. In July 1985, CSX announced that the Cumberland–Cincinnati route would lose its mainline status, and on August 31, the last through freights graced the Parkersburg Line. In addition to silencing the Parkersburg Branch, this ended most through traffic that traversed the historic B&O West End. The legendary Cranberry and Seventeen Mile Grades were reduced to the status of a coal funnel. In addition to coal drags, a single pair of merchandise trains remained on the historic route between Cumberland and Grafton.

The last sunlight of April 6, 2004, illuminates a CSX eastward freight running along Route 20 near Huntington, Massachusetts. *Brian Solomon*

Right: During the 1980s, CSX trimmed its route map by selling and abandoning several routes. Among the lines sold were the former B&O Buffalo, Rochester & Pittsburgh routes. In 1986, the old BR&P 4th Subdivision was conveyed to Genesee & Wyoming's Rochester & Southern, which operated between Rochester, New York, and Ashford Junction, with running rights to the yard at East Salamanca, New York. Two years later, the G&W railroad family took control of most remaining BR&P lines and operated them as the Buffalo & Pittsburgh. *Brian Solomon*

Above: Northward Rochester & Southern freight passes Ronzo's Grocery at Garbutt, New York. With the sale of the former BR&P line to Rochester, New York, to Genesee & Wyoming's R&S, CSX effectively exited the Rochester market, but still maintained a friendly connection. In the early 1990s, poor track conditions led R&S to abandon most of the line south of Silver Springs, New York. *Brian Solomon*

In 1986, CSX applied to the ICC to abandon 61 miles of the Parkersburg Branch. Two years later the rails were lifted. CSX had severed the route of B&O's famous *National Limited.* Unfortunately, while this move may have fulfilled short-term financial objectives, it cut America's most direct all-rail route between Baltimore and St. Louis. This line had enjoyed a major clearance improvement project in the early 1960s, and would have been ideally suited for the transport of high-clearance double-stack container trains, as well as unit grain trains moving from the Midwest to the port of Baltimore. This abandonment is often cited as one of the errors of railroad management in the 1980s. It was cut just before the swell of traffic made possible by the Staggers Act began to overwhelm American railroads. The tragic irony in this case is that Harley O. Staggers, who drafted the Act, was a Congressman from West Virginia. In the 1970s, he exerted political pressure for Amtrak to operate a train over the Parkersburg Branch.

Another once busy, but vastly under-utilized portion of the B&O system was the former BR&P lines. In the summer of 1986, CSX sold the operation of the 96-mile former BR&P 4th Subdivision between Rochester and Ashford Junction to Genesee & Wyoming's Rochester & Southern. This line suffered from years of neglect described in industry terms as "deferred maintenance." Much of the line was saddled with serious speed restrictions that limited operations to 10 and 20 miles per hour. Then two years later, following months of negotiations, CSX conveyed

Above: In July 1988 after months of negotiation, the BR&P route between Buffalo, New York, and Eidenau, Pennsylvania (plus trackage rights on CSX's P&W Subdivision to the yard at New Castle), was conveyed to Genesee & Wyoming's newly formed Buffalo & Pittsburgh. This train, photographed on July 19, 1988, north of Ashford Junction, New York, was the first northward B&P through freight. B&P's own locomotives were not yet available for service, so CSX power was used. *Brian Solomon*

Left: The first Buffalo & Pittsburgh train rolls north of Ashford Junction on the old B&O Buffalo, Rochester & Pittsburgh route to Buffalo, New York, on July 19, 1988. *Brian Solomon*

A southward freight crosses the immense former Atlantic Coast Line bridge over the James River at Richmond, Virginia, on February 16, 2004. *Brian Solomon*

most of the remaining BR&P lines to Buffalo & Pittsburgh, another new G&W controlled firm. This transaction consisted of 373 miles of line between Buffalo and East Salamanca, New York, and Eidenau, Pennsylvania, with trackage rights to CSX's yard at New Castle, Pennsylvania. Prior to the sale, this had been the route of B&O's *Empire State Special,* a priority merchandise freight to Buffalo that carried the ESSP symbol. Buffalo & Pittsburgh was one of many new regional railroads—lines with more than 300 route miles—created by Class I spin-offs in the 1980s.

CSX strategists continued to nip away at the B&O. It is no wonder that Jervis Langdon Jr. expressed dismay at the dismemberment of his railroad. By late 2004, a great deal of the old B&O network had been trimmed, with the notable exception of its principal Philadelphia–Washington, D.C., and Baltimore to Chicago trunks. When CSX announced it wanted to cut as much as 4,000 miles from its 23,000-mile system in mid-2004, it put the old West End and coal feeders in the Grafton area on the block. As of this writing in late 2004, that route had yet to be sold.

The old Seaboard Air Line route structure hasn't faired well either. In the late 1980s, most of the S line—what operating people call the old Seaboard main—between Petersburg, Virginia, and Raleigh, North Carolina, was downgraded and portions were abandoned. Generally speaking. Seaboard's north-south routes north of Jacksonville have been eclipsed in favor of former ACL routes. By contrast, SAL's east-west lines remain largely integral to CSX operations.

The Monon and Western Maryland have been dismembered and largely abandoned or downgraded. Both lines were essentially parallel to other CSX routes and viewed as redundant. A few portions of the Monon still see through traffic, but the line is no longer contiguous, and most of its Indianapolis and

Michigan City lines are gone. Likewise, the vast majority of the Western Maryland Railway is a subject best studied by industrial archeologists except for the Cherry Run to Baltimore route and a few branches in western Maryland. Its bridges, tunnels, and cuttings are testimony to railroad mogul George Gould's early twentieth-century ambitions to assemble a transcontinental railroad empire, but they play no useful role in modern CSX operations. The once busy hump at Hagerstown is silent, WM's Connellsville extension just an impressive curiosity, and its legendary grade to Elkins just a trail in the woods.

The old C&O has not been exempt from rationalization. As mentioned in Chapter 1, most of C&O's lightly used Cincinnati to Chicago route was lifted in the mid-1980s. More recently, C&O's original line from Richmond to Clifton Forge via Doswell, Charlottesville, and over the Blue Ridge was among those put up for sale in 2004. Arrangements have been made to lease this historic line to the Buckingham Branch Railroad, which will assume operation and track and bridge maintenance.

The trimming of CSX's network reflects changes in transportation across its territory. At one time it would have been unthinkable to cut important lines such as the B&O West End or C&O's mainline, but today these changes reflect the decline in importance of the coal and merchandise carried on these routes.

Not all of the changes reflect retrenchment. Today, one of the busiest routes on CSX is the old B&O west of Greenwich, Ohio, to Chicago. In preparation for the Conrail split, CSX invested millions to expand the capacity of its B&O route west of the connection with NYC's Big Four route at Greenwich. It restored double track west of Deshler, Ohio, which had been reduced to single track during the mid-1980s. In 2000, the old B&O was one of the heaviest trunk lines into Chicago and carried an estimated 105 million ton-miles annually.

Two AC4400CWs lead a loaded coal train bound for a southern power utility across the Copper Creek viaduct at twilight on the former Clinchfield Railroad KP Subdivision on March 22, 2004. This nearly quarter-mile-long viaduct near Speers Ferry, Virginia, lifts the former Clinchfield over the valley formed by Copper Creek where the creek meets the Clinch River in rural southwestern Virginia. ***T. S. Hoover***

At Acca Yard in Richmond, Virginia, a lineup of inherited CSX locomotives displays the variety of the railroad's fleet. From left to right: 7015 is a General Electric C30-7 built in 1979 for Louisville & Nashville in the Family Lines era; 6241 is a GP40-2 built in 1979; 9651 is a former C&O GP38 painted for maintenance of way service; 8148 is an SD40-2 built in 1981. *Tim Doherty*

CHAPTER THREE

CSX LOCOMOTIVES

Heritage Fleet

When CSX was created in 1980, its respective railroads continued to maintain independent locomotive fleets. It wasn't until after the creation of CSX Transportation in 1986 that locomotives from Chessie and Seaboard System fleets began to routinely operate across the entire CSX system. The different fleets reflected the buying practices of the individual railroads, and there was a great variety of models in service across the system.

Chesapeake & Ohio operated a major freight yard in Russell, Kentucky. Traditionally, this was a primary facility for marshalling coal traffic, the mainstay of C&O's freight business. Switching the yard at Russell is one of C&O's unusual Electro-Motive Division SD18s that rode on Alco tri-mount trucks recovered from traded-in RSD-5s. *George Pitarys*

CSX's component railroads had been slow to paint locomotives, so with the introduction of the first CSXT-painted locomotives in early 1986, there were already about a dozen paint schemes worn by CSX locomotives. In addition to Chessie System, Seaboard System, and Family Lines paint liveries, locomotives wore paint from various B&O, C&O, WM, SCL, L&N, Clinchfield, and Georgia Railroad schemes.

Chessie System

Since the late 1950s, B&O had only purchased new General Motors' Electro-Motive Division products, and the sounds of 16-567 and 16-645 engines were alive across the railroad. In 1981, the railroad's fleet consisted of large numbers of four-axle Electro-Motive road units that ranged from switchers to 1950s-era GP7s and GP9s and modern 3,000-horsepower GP40-2s. B&O had been an early buyer of six-motor diesels, and at the beginning of CSX, it had a modest roster of six-motor locomotives, including 5 SD7s, 10 SD9s, 15 SD35s, 8 SD40s, and 20 SD40-2s. In general, B&O had preferred four-motor units for merchandise freight and intermodal trains and assigned six-motor units to coal trains in graded territory. For many years, its SD35 fleet worked helper assignments on the West End between Keyser and Grafton, West Virginia.

By 1981, WM, like B&O, was an all Electro-Motive railroad, although WM had once owned a sizeable fleet of Alco RS-3 and FAs. As Western Maryland's operations were melded with B&O's during the 1970s, it became common to find WM's red-and-white or black-and-gold diesels mixed in with B&O's. WM's late-era roster of 110 units resembled a scaled-down version of B&O's

The first CSX AC4400CW, road number 1, leads southbound loaded coal train W624-30 on the KP (Kingsport) Subdivision near McClure, Virginia, on January 31, 2004. The train is framed in tunnel No. 18, the short 412-foot Caney Fork tunnel. Because of the difficult terrain and the Clinchfield Railroad's high engineering standards for gentle curves and grades, the former Clinchfield Elkhorn Extension has 21 tunnels between Elkhorn City, Kentucky, and Dante, Virginia. In modern CSX operations, southbound loaded coal trains require a two-unit DASH 8-40CW helper on the rear as far as the summit of the Alleghenies at Sandy Ridge tunnel. *T. S. Hoover*

and was dominated by four-motor GP7s, GP9s, GP35s, and GP40/GP40-2s. It had just 17 six-motor units, 5 SD35s, and 12 SD40s. By this time it no longer had traditional switchers but continued to operate a pair of BL2s built in 1948. These unusual units were paired with home-built slugs and assigned to the Hagerstown Hump. One of WM's preserved BL2s is now displayed at the B&O Railroad Museum in Baltimore, along with other significant diesels, including a B&O GP40 and the first E unit, B&O model EA number 51.

Coal-hauling C&O did not begin dieselization in earnest until 1949, and as a result it purchased a large number of GP7s and GP9s, and almost 350 remained on the property in 1981. Likewise, it also had a modest fleet of Electro-Motive switchers purchased between 1949 and 1952, and more than 70 were still active at the time of CSX's creation in 1980. Its road fleet included dozens of GP30s, GP35s, GP38s, and GP40s, plus 95 GP40-2s that were bought between 1972 and 1980. It had 20 GP39s built in 1969, which used a turbocharged 12-cylinder

Opposite above: In 1985, as new high-horsepower SD50s were being delivered, Chessie System stored dozens of older locomotives. At Cumberland, Maryland, in May 1985, the deadline consists of GP9s and other old Electro-Motive products; many were still dressed in the paint schemes of Chessie's predecessors. *Brian Solomon*

Opposite below: In May 1985, a westward freight departs the B&O yard at Cumberland, Maryland, behind a mixed consist of four-axle EMDs. In the lead is GP40-2 4829 sub-lettered for C&O, followed by GP30 6954 sub-lettered for B&O. A GP40 and GP9 are trailing, and both are still wearing the pre-Chessie System B&O blue. A few B&O blue units survived well into the CSX era. *Brian Solomon*

An Alco C628 leads a westward Louisville & Nashville caboose hop at Loyall, Kentucky, on October 7, 1979. L&N was one of only a handful of railroads to purchase C628s. Only 135 C628s were built for railroads in the United States. This locomotive wears the 1970s-era Family Lines livery, while the C420s in the distance feature an L&N paint scheme. *Jeremy F. Plant*

Chessie System
WM
6834

C&O
4829
Chessie System
Chessie System
B&O

The Electro-Motive GP9 was a workhorse model on Chessie System predecessors. The GP9 was one of the best-selling diesels of all time. This locomotive, built in the mid-1950s, used the reliable 16-567C engine and produced 1,750 horsepower. GP9s were "General Purpose" locomotives and assigned to a variety of services from switching and local freight work to heavy freight and passenger duties. This machine was still hard at work in the mid-1980s. *Brian Solomon*

A detailed view of CSX FP7 118, one of four former Clinchfield Fs that survived into modern-day CSX. These Fs have since been retired from the roster. Three now work on a tourist railroad in West Virginia. *Brian Solomon*

645 to produce 2,300 horsepower. It also had a fair roster of six-motor Electro-Motive units, including a dozen SD35s and more than 60 SD40s. Perhaps the most unusual diesels on C&O were its 19 SD18s, which rode on recycled Alco tri-mount trucks from traded-in RSD-5s. These trucks used GE traction motors and as a result had a 74:18 gear ratio, which was common on Alco and GE products but unusual on Electro-Motive's, which typically used a 62:15 gear ratio. In addition to its large numbers of Electro-Motive products, Chesapeake & Ohio was the only Chessie System road to buy General Electric diesels.

C&O had long been a General Electric user and bought a fleet of GE's pioneering U25B road diesels in 1963 and 1964. While all 38 of C&O's U25Bs were off the roster by 1981, it operated four General Electric models: 13 U30Cs built in 1967 and 1968; 30 U23Bs built in 1969; 35 U30Bs built in 1972; and 44 B30-7s (from GE's improved line introduced in 1977 to supplant its Universal Line) built between 1978 and 1980. In 1986, one of the first exchanges between Chessie and Seaboard was the conveyance of all C&O GEs to Seaboard territory in exchange for Seaboard System GP40s. This simplified the parts supply and maintenance because the Seaboard System already had large fleets of GEs on both former SCL and L&N lines that were maintained at Waycross, Georgia, and Corbin, Kentucky.

Prior to the consolidation of its railroads under the CSX Transportation umbrella in 1986, CSX began coordinating a locomotive acquisition. An order for 144 SD50s built between 1983 and 1985 was divided between Chessie System and Seaboard System, and each received appropriately painted locomotives that were sequentially numbered from 8500 to 8643—numbers they have retained throughout their CSX operation. During 1982, C&O bought 25 GP15-1s, a road-switcher model that used a turbocharged 8-cylinder 645 engine to produce 1,500 horsepower.

Family Lines and Seaboard System

The locomotives that were painted with Family Lines paint were still owned and maintained by their respective railroads. Locomotives were gradually renumbered into a common roster, and individual locomotives were sub-lettered for owning railroads.

By the advent of CSX, Georgia Railroad and its affiliates, Atlanta & West Point and Western Railway of Alabama, had small rosters of four-motor Electro-Motive diesels. Prior to adopting the Family Lines livery, these lines used an uninspired basic black scheme. With 38 locomotives, Georgia had the largest fleet of the three lines. Half of its locomotives were venerable GP7s. Its newest diesels were four GP38-2s that were built in

At Cumberland, Maryland, in May 1985, a relatively new Chessie System SD50 leads a loaded coal train that originated in Grafton, West Virginia. Difficulties with the SD50 design soured CSX to Electro-Motive products, and for the next dozen years the railroad primarily ordered General Electric products. ***Brian Solomon***

Right: In the 1970s, many railroads painted and numbered locomotives to honor the U.S. bicentennial. Seaboard Coast Line No. 1776 was a new General Electric–built U36B that was delivered in July 1971. It is displayed in St. Petersburg, Florida, on August 12, 1971. *R.R. Richardson, Doug Eisele collection*

Below: New Seaboard System SD50s pause with an empty coal train on the old Georgia Railroad at Avondale near Decatur in suburban Atlanta, Georgia, in May 1985. The SD50 was introduced in 1981 and produced through the end of 1985. The model boosted the output of General Motor's standard six-motor locomotive from 3,000 horsepower to 3,500 horsepower using the 16-645F engine. CSX's component railroads, Chessie System and Seaboard System, were two of the largest purchasers of the model. Unfortunately reliability issues plagued the SD50 and the model was superceded by the SD60 in the mid-1980s. *Brian Solomon*

1979 and 1981. Atlanta & West Point had just 12 locomotives: 2 GP38-2s, 2 GP7s, 7 GP40s, and 1 GP40-2. Western Railway of Alabama had six GP7s, two GP9s, two GP38s, seven GP40s, and one GP40-2.

In the 1950s, Clinchfield replaced its steam fleet with Electro-Motive F units, GP7s, and switchers. Interestingly, four of its F units survived in active service well into the CSX era and worked in their later years on executive passenger trains, and for about a year on CSX's Detroit–Atlanta RoadRailer trains. In addition to the surviving handfuls of Fs, GPs, and switchers, the majority of Clinchfield's locomotives were six-motor units. In the CSX era Clinchfield was an all Electro-Motive railroad; however, between 1971 and 1977 it operated seven U36Cs, which were ultimately traded to SCL for an equal quantity of SD45s. It also had 25

The brand-new Seaboard Coast Line MP15AC 4215 catches the sun at Collier Yard, south of Petersburg, Virginia. Both Louisville & Nashville and SCL ordered these GM Electro-Motive Division 1,500 switchers in the late 1970s. Now numbered in the 1100 series, most were still at work on CSX in late 2004. ***Doug Riddell***

CSX predecessors B&O and C&O bought large numbers of GP30s, and many served CSX in their later years. CSX 4226 had been C&O GP30 No. 3035 and is seen here in the early CSX blue and gray livery. Most CSX GP30s were rebuilt in the 1980s and designated GP30Ms. Since this photo was made in July 1988, all of CSX's GP30Ms have been retired. The last was retired in 1997, but some of the locomotives have been converted into road slugs and paired with another locomotive. *Brian Solomon*

SD40s, 6 SD40-2s, and 18 SD45-2s. High-horsepower six-motor diesels were ideal to move the line's heavy coal trains over its graded Appalachian route. Prior to Family Lines paint, Clinchfield dressed its locomotives in black with gold lettering, a scheme remarkably similar to that of SCL.

Louisville & Nashville had the most diverse and arguably the most eclectic modern fleet of all CSX predecessors. In 1980, it had more than 30 different models and was the only CSX railroad to operate road locomotives from Alco, GE, and Electro-Motive. At that time it had more than 90 Alco road diesels, including RS11s, C420s, C430s, C628s, and C630s. In the early 1980s, it was among the last large railroads in the United States that still used Alcos in heavy freight service. Its significant General Electric fleet, which until 1984 included the last intact original roster of U25Bs, looked something like a GE Universal Line catalog. It included U23Bs, U28Bs, U30Bs, U25Cs, U28Cs, and U30Cs. Many of these models survived well into the CSX era. L&N also bought B23-7s and C30-7s. A variety of switchers, including NW2s, SW7s, and SW9s, and modern SW1500s and MP15ACs, were among L&N's numerous Electro-Motive diesels. It

had dozens of GP7s and GP9s, plus four GP18s. High-horsepower four-motor units included GP30s, GP35s, and GP40s, as well as 2,000-horsepower GP38s and GP38ACs. It had 20 SD35s, 25 SDP35s, and almost 3 dozen SD40s. Two of L&N's most numerous types were GP38-2s and SD40-2s. In addition to locomotives that were bought new, L&N's fleet included those inherited from Monon and Chicago & Eastern Illinois.

Seaboard Coast Line was another significant General Electric customer. It bought large numbers of four-motor GEs, including more than 100 high-horsepower U36Bs for use on its Atlantic Coast Line raceway. It also

The SD40-2 was considered the standard freight locomotive of the 1970s and early 1980s. Although less numerous on CSX properties than some western railroads, the SD40-2 can still be found on CSX lines. In March 2004, CSX SD40-2 8427 leads a northward freight crossing Big Creek Trestle at Ivydale, Tennessee, a few miles north of Lafollette, on the former Louisville & Nashville CC Subdivision, now CSX's KD Subdivision. *Marshall W. Beecher*

had a handful of U30Cs, plus the above-mentioned seven U36Cs received in trade from Clinchfield. SCL was one of three railroads in the United States to buy GE's 1,800-horsepower U18B, which used an 8-cylinder version of the FDL engine. While moderately powered GEs were popular for export, they only saw limited application in the United States. SCL had by far the largest fleet that consisted of 105 units. Some of SCL's GEs rode on recycled Blomberg trucks, and others were on GE's own Floating Bolster trucks. The most unusual-looking GEs on the roster were 10 BQ23-7s—a unique variation of the more common 2,250-horsepower B23-7. These featured oversized boxy cabs to accommodate extra crew space on caboose-less trains prior to the reduction of crew sizes in the mid-1980s. SCL also bought several dozen ordinary B23-7s and six-motor C30-7s. SCL's preference for high-horsepower four-motor GEs continued into the Seaboard System era with purchases of both B30-7s and B36-7s. One of the more unusual motive power purchases were the General Electric MATEs that SCL bought in 1971 and 1972 to operate with its GE four-motor diesels working in moderate-speed heavy tonnage service, specifically for its phosphate operations in central Florida. A MATE is essentially a road slug that is capable of higher speeds than a typical yard slug, and also carries a fuel tank for the locomotive it is paired with. (A slug is a non-powered unit equipped with traction motors and ballast designed for operation with a locomotive to provide greater tractive effort in slow-speed applications.)

In 1980, SCL still had an eclectic collection of vintage switchers, including a handful of Baldwins and Alcos that had been re-equipped with Electro-Motive engines. Unlike many railroads that had largely given up on switchers by the late 1970s, SCL continued to order Electro-Motive switchers, and during 1977 and 1978, it bought 45 MP15ACs. These locomotives used a different airflow arrangement than traditional Electro-Motive switchers with featured side air intake vents at the end of the hood near the running boards. Seaboard System continued to buy switchers in the 1980s, and bought 41 of Electro-Motive's MP15T model, which was nearly all of this model's production. Like C&O's GP15Ts, Seaboard's MP15T used a turbocharged 8-cylinder 645 engine instead of the 12-cylinder 645 with a Roots blower that was more commonly used on Electro-Motive 1,500-horsepower switchers. SCL's Electro-Motive diesels included GP7s, GP9s, GP18s, GP30s, GP35s, GP38-2s, GP40s, GP40-2s, SD35s, SD40-2s, SD45s, and SD45-2s. Numerous older GP7s and GP9s were rebuilt at company shops into 1,600-horsepower road-switchers with low short hoods and designated as GP16s.

The Modern CSX Fleet

Since CSX Transportation assumed operation of its various predecessors, it has largely ordered high-horsepower six-motor road diesels. In 1989, it received 10 Electro-Motive SD60s, numbered 8700 to 8709. The relatively poor performance of its SD50s, followed by the less-than-ideal performance of these SD60s, and Seaboard System's long-standing penchant for GE product contributed to CSX's preference for new General Electric diesels over the next dozen years.

General Electric DASH 8

In the early 1980s, General Electric made a major business commitment by advancing diesel-electric technology with the development of onboard microprocessor controls for use on its new DASH 8 line. Locomotive electrical control systems had utilized advances in technology and gradually progressed from traditional relay controls to solid-state electronic modules to, finally, microprocessors. The DASH 8 used an improved version of GE's proven 16-cylinder FDL diesel engine, the same basic powerplant that the company had relied on since the introduction of the U25B 30 years earlier. By employing microprocessor control, GE refined locomotive component performance in order to improve fuel efficiency, reliability, and enhance overall performance.

In 1989, CSX ordered its first DASH 8s, six-motor 4,000-horsepower DASH 8-40Cs, and by the end of 1990, it had 147 of them numbered 7500 to 7646. CSX's DASH 8-40Cs, which were designated C40-8 (in order to remain more consistent with GE's older model scheme), featured high-capacity fuel tanks and provided each unit with 5,000 gallons of diesel fuel. This allowed the railroad to assign the locomotives to unusually long runs without the need for refueling. Among their earliest regular assignments were on coal trains originating in Kentucky and Virginia destined for Florida. A DASH 8-40C could make a full cycle from Corbin, Kentucky, to Florida and return without refueling. Other early assignments included Chicago–Waycross, Georgia, and Detroit–Waycross. The DASH 8-40C's

Above: Seaboard System bought General Electric B36-7s for priority intermodal service. They have been bumped to less demanding duties and are routinely assigned to local freights. On May 29, 2004, a pair of consecutively numbered B36-7s lead a local freight down the former Conrail Hudson Line near Hudson, New York. This was once the route of New York Central's famous *Twentieth Century Limited* and still hosts many Amtrak trains. Most CSX freight moving to the New York City area travels via the River Line on the West Shore of the Hudson to North Jersey terminals. *Brian Solomon*

Right: The engineer in B36-7 5831 on May 29, 2004. *Brian Solomon*

A former C&O SD40-2 and a GP38 lead a westward train with coiled steel cars west of Fostoria, Ohio, on the B&O during the morning of July 22, 1988. This SD40-2 was painted in the early CSX blue and gray livery. Later CSX paint schemes featured yellow ends. The 3,000-horsepower SD40-2 is highly regarded by locomotive engineers. Both SD40 and SD40-2 models were purchased by CSX predecessor lines. *Brian Solomon*

Leading a southward freight on the old Atlantic Coast Line mainline at Weldon, North Carolina, is a former Conrail SD60I. During the mid-1990s Conrail assembled SD60Is using components supplied by General Motors at the former Pennsylvania Railroad shops in Altoona, Pennsylvania. *Brian Solomon*

high reliability and performance made them ideal for all types of service, and by mid-1990, many were working in merchandise service and typically replaced GP40 and GP40-2 locomotives.

In 1990, CSX acquired 20 4,000-horsepower four-motor DASH 8-40Bs from New York, Susquehanna & Western. In 1989, CSX had helped NYS&W finance these locomotives when that line was designated operator of the Delaware & Hudson. NYS&W forwarded CSX/Sea-Land container traffic to its intermodal terminal at Little Ferry, New Jersey. Although NYS&W made a bid to purchase D&H, Canadian Pacific bought D&H in the 1990s so NYS&W no longer needed these nearly new DASH 8-40Bs. CSX renumbered them 5930–5949, which followed logically after its B36-7 block of 5806–5925. Until the Conrail acquisition in 1999, these were CSX's only four-motor DASH 8s. With Conrail, CSX got another 12 DASH 8-40Bs, which were numbered 5950 to 5961.

During the late 1980s, Santa Fe had worked with both General Electric and Electro-Motive to design a safer, more comfortable, and more ergonomic locomotive cab. Based in part on Canadian designs, both locomotive builders began offering wide-nose safety cabs as an option on new locomotives. CSX ordered its first safety cabs from GE in the second quarter of 1991. These were 53 DASH 40-CWs, numbered 7650 to 7702,

In September 1989, a pair of brand-new General Electric DASH 8-40Cs lead a southward freight on the old B&O at Deshler, Ohio. CSX predecessors Seaboard Coast Line and Louisville & Nashville had both been large General Electric customers. With the introduction of the microprocessor-controlled DASH 8 models in the late 1980s, CSX made a large investment in GE locomotives. The DASH 8 has proven to be a reliable line and a significant improvement over earlier GE locomotive models. ***Brian Solomon***

which CSX designated CW40-8s. Since this purchase, all new CSX locomotives have safety cabs. Over the next two years, CSX ordered another 215 DASH 8-40CWs that were numbered sequentially from 7703 to 7917. In late 1993, CSX received three experimental hybrid locomotives numbered 9000 to 9002 that featured electronic fuel injection (EFI) and produced a slightly higher output of 4,380 horsepower. Since they embodied some of the characteristics of GE's new DASH 9 line, including EFI, CSX designated these locomotives CW44-9. However, these locomotives did not feature some equipment that was considered standard with the DASH 9, such as GE's recently introduced Hi-Ad truck. Fifty additional CW44-9s, numbered 9003 to 9052, were built in the first quarter of 1994.

Conrail was another large operator of modern GE locomotives, and with CSX's acquisition of approximately 40 percent of the Conrail fleet, CSX inherited more than 100 six-motor DASH 8s. In addition to the aforementioned DASH 8-40Bs, there were also late-era DASH 7s in the form of 3,000-horsepower C30-7As and 3,600-horsepower C36-7s. Many of these locomotives operated in Conrail paint with CSX numbers for a number of years after June 1, 1999. The most common were DASH 8-40CWs numbered in the 7300 series.

With the split of Conrail, CSX inherited many former Conrail locomotives. CSX 7381 is a General Electric DASH 8-40CW, a 4,000-horsepower locomotive built for Conrail in 1994. It leads an eastward freight through the old Union Station in Springfield, Massachusetts, on the former Boston & Albany route in March 2003. *Brian Solomon*

On a frigid January 2001 morning, a pair of CSX AC6000CWs rest at West Springfield Yard in West Springfield, Massachusetts. CSX and Union Pacific were the only railroads to acquire the AC6000CW. These powerful locomotives use the HDL engine that was developed by German manufacturer Deutz MWM. Beginning in 2000, CSX routinely assigned many of its AC6000CWs to former Conrail lines radiating from its yard in Selkirk, New York. These locomotives have been routinely used in pairs on the old Boston & Albany route. *Tim Doherty*

General Electric Alternating Current Traction

In the early 1990s, CSX wanted a more economical solution for movement of coal in heavily graded territory. Developments in Europe using modern three-phase alternating current traction had paved the way for American application of this technology for heavy-haul applications. The inherent motor characteristics of three-phase AC motors make them virtually free from the overheating that plagues DC motors when operating at maximum load. Where DC-traction locomotives are limited by short-time motor ratings to keep motors from overheating when operating at maximum load, AC locomotives can operate at maximum load at virtually any speed with minimal risk of motor damage or stalling. In addition, three-phase AC motors offer greatly improved wheel-slip control and extended range dynamic braking, both of which aid in operating heavy trains in graded territory while reducing costs. Burlington Northern and Electro-Motive worked together in the development of AC traction to move Powder River Basin coal. General Electric followed Electro-Motive's lead when CSX made a serious commitment to purchase large numbers of GE ACs.

General Electric delivered the first AC4400CWs to CSX in the fourth quarter of 1994. Similar in appearance to late-era DASH 8/DASH 9s, these locomotives could be easily distinguished by the extra-large box on the fireman's (left) side of the locomotive used to house inverters—banks of high-tech electrical equipment that convert direct current to a form of three-phase alternating current for traction—and the use of lightning bolts on either side of the road numbers painted on

Two AC4400CWs lead a loaded coal train bound for a southern utility across the Copper Creek viaduct on the former Clinchfield Railroad KP Subdivision on March 22, 2004. The nearly quarter-mile-long viaduct near Speers Ferry, Virginia, lifts the former Clinchfield over the valley formed by Copper Creek where it meets the Clinch River in rural southwestern Virginia. *T. S. Hoover*

cab sides. Since 1994, CSX has purchased 594 AC4400CWs and made this the most common model on the modern CSX roster. They are numbered from 1 to 173, 201 to 599, and 5101 to 5122. The initial AC4400s came with GE's Hi-Ad truck, and following experiments in mid-1996, the later locomotives were delivered with GE's steerable truck, which is designed to improve adhesion and reduce wheel-wear in curves.

Following GE's success with the AC4400CW, CSX and Union Pacific expressed interest in the development of an even more powerful GE AC-traction locomotive. GE's old FDL engine had reached the limit of its practical output; to build a more powerful locomotive GE teamed up with the German engine manufacturer Deutz MWM to build a new diesel engine. This engine is known as GE 7HDL and, like the 7FDL, it is a four-cycle design. It was used to power the AC6000CW, which uses a significantly larger carbody than the AC4400CW and features much larger radiators than any earlier GE locomotive.

The most powerful locomotives on CSX are General Electric AC6000CWs built between 1998 and 2000. Rated at 6,000 horsepower, these locomotives were designed to allow for a two-for-one replacement of older locomotives. On the Boston & Albany route, a pair of AC6000CWs replaced four 1980s-era General Electric C30-7As. The AC6000CWs can be identified by the larger carbody and the larger radiators than earlier GE designs. The massive wings at the rear of the locomotive house the radiators that can accommodate 550 gallons of coolant. ***Brian Solomon***

Interrupting the bliss of Virginia's Leesylvania State Park is a northward CSX freight on the former RF&P mainline led by No. 699, built as an AC6000CW and later experimentally retrofitted with a 16-cylinder FDL engine rated at 4,400 horsepower. It was one of several locomotives that carries a banner reading "CSX Diversity in Motion." Note the locomotive's larger radiators in comparison with the 1980s-era DASH 8-40C trailing behind it. *Brian Solomon*

Massive wings at the rear of the locomotive house the radiators that are designed to accommodate 550 gallons of coolant. Three prototype AC6000CWs, numbered 600 to 602, were delivered to CSX in September 1996. At the B&O Railroad Museum in Baltimore on September 13, 1996, No. 602 posed with the historic oversized replica of Peter Cooper's 1830 locomotive to celebrate the inauguration of AC6000CW service. The other two were already being tested in coal servicing during the inauguration. Additional AC6000CWs were delivered to CSX in the fourth quarter of 1998, and by the middle of 2000, GE had delivered 117 AC6000CWs to CSX, which was the majority of total production. These are numbered 600 to 699, and 5001 to 5016. According to the May 1999 *CTC Board*, initially the production AC6000CWs were assigned to intermodal service out of Jacksonville, Florida. They worked trains to Tampa, Florida, as well as Q141-Q142 between Jacksonville and Cincinnati, and the Q101-102 and Q105-Q106 Jacksonville–New Orleans intermodal runs. In mid-2000,

CSX represents a great contrast in railroad technology. In February 2003, one of CSX's newest locomotives, a General Electric AC6000CW, passes one of the oldest signal installations in North America at the mechanical, non-interlocked crossing at Brighton Park in Chicago. The lightning bolts on either side of the road number indicate the locomotive uses three-phase AC-traction motors. *Brian Solomon*

many of the AC6000s had been assigned to former Conrail lines based out of Selkirk, New York. CSX has had a mixed response to the AC6000CW. In 2002, CSX looked to de-rate some of its big locomotives. No. 699 was physically altered by exchanging a 4,400-horsepower FDL engine for the HDL. Other locomotives were temporarily de-rated through software modifications. With additional effort from GE and CSX, all AC6000CWs have been returned to the original 6,000-horsepower rating and their assignments on intermodal and merchandise trains as of this writing.

CSX GP38-2 2625 on Easter Sunday 1988. CSX inherited numerous four-axle locomotives from its predecessors. Four-axle, moderate-horsepower locomotives such as the GP38/GP38-2 and GE-built B23-7 were routinely assigned to local freights and switching duties. *Brian Solomon*

A billboard in Cumberland, Maryland, introduces CSX's first AC-traction General Motors diesels, the SD70MAC. GM's Electro-Motive Division developed the SD70MAC with its three-phase alternating current traction system for Burlington Northern in the early 1990s at the same time General Electric was working with CSX in the development of the AC4400CW. In 1997, CSX ordered 25 SD70MACs and assigned them to coal service out of Cumberland, Maryland. *William M. Beecher Jr.*

Against a backdrop of splendid autumn foliage, CSX SD70MAC 4723 leads eastward intermodal train Q116 at Warren, Massachusetts, on October 11, 2004. Since they were first delivered, the 4700-series SD70MACs have been regularly operated over the former Boston & Albany route. *Brian Solomon*

Electro-Motive AC Traction

In 1997, after more than a decade since it had placed a substantial order for Electro-Motive diesels, CSX ordered 25 SD70MACs. This was the model that had been developed for Burlington Northern for its Powder River coal traffic. These were based at Cumberland, Maryland, and assigned coal-traffic moving over the old West End. These were numbered 700 to 724, and like the GE ACs, they can be distinguished from the similar DC-traction locomotives by the lightning bolts on either side of the road number. The class leader, No. 700, was named the *Spirit of Cumberland* in October 1997. Additional orders for new SD70MACs, plus 15 locomotives, were ordered by CSX, but were delivered to Conrail and brought CSX's fleet to 90 units by the end of 2000. The Conrail merger also added 12 5,000-horsepower SD80MACs to CSX's AC fleet.

In 2003 and 2004, CSX ordered a more modern variation of the SD70MAC that featured angled rear radiators to accommodate

In October 2004, CSX SD70MAC 4722 catches the late afternoon sun near Middlefield, Massachusetts, as it ascends the east slope of Washington Hill with a very heavy westward freight. *Brian Solomon*

Above: A pair of AC4400CWs lead a southward train at Grant Park, Illinois, on June 5, 2004. This former Chicago & Eastern Illinois trackage is now owned by Union Pacific with CSX trackage rights to Chicago. These locomotives wear CSX's latest livery, which is reminiscent of the 1960s-era Chesapeake & Ohio scheme. *Brian Solomon*

Opposite top: An AC4400CW leads a southward empty coal train and crosses a wooden trestle on CSX's E&BU Subdivision at Deane, Kentucky, in October 1999. By 2002, CSX had bought nearly 600 General Electric AC4400CWs and made this model by far the most common modern type in CSX's road fleet. Significantly, CSX has not purchased a new direct current traction locomotive since it began acquiring AC4400CWs in the third quarter of 1993. All its new locomotives use modern three-phase alternating current traction motors. *William M. Beecher, Jr.*

Opposite bottom: A picture of modern power. On May 29, 2004, CSX GE AC4400CW 588 and Electro-Motive SD70MAC 4723 lead a westward freight across the bridge at French's Hollow in Guilderland, New York. The AC4400CW is from CSX's most recent GE order that was delivered in late 2002, while the SD70MAC is among CSX's most modern GM locomotives and features larger radiator capacity to reduce gas emissions. *Brian Solomon*

increased radiator capacity for improved greenhouse gas emissions. They were delivered in the new CSX livery that was introduced in 2002 and consisted of a dark blue body color with mustard orange ends that resembled the 1960s-era C&O/B&O livery and contrasted with the 1990s-era Bright Future blue, gray, and banana yellow scheme. By late 2004, CSX had 130 of these modern SD70MACs that were numbered 4701 to 4730. CSX's most recent order from Electro-Motive was for 20 state-of-the-art SD70ACs, numbered 4731 to 4750.

The Conrail acquisition brought a host of older Electro-Motive DC-traction models to CSX, including GP15-1s, GP38-2s, GP40-2s, SD40-2s, SD50s, SD60, SD60M, and SD60Is. The latter two models are significant because CSX had not owned any Electro-Motive DC-traction safety cabs until it acquired these Conrail types.

377
CSX

4723
CSX
CSX
588

Road Slugs

Between 1988 and 1998, CSX contracted for the conversion of approximately 150 older four-motor Electro-Motive diesels, mostly GP30s and GP35s, to be rebuilt as road slugs. As in the case of the General Electric–built MATEs described earlier, these units were designed to be paired with a locomotive to provide additional tractive effort. Unlike the MATEs and most yard slugs, these road slugs looked similar to ordinary locomotives. The engines and related equipment were removed and replaced with ballast, while external features such as radiator grilles and most air intakes and fans were removed and blanked up. Electrical equipment such as traction motors and dynamic brake equipment were left in place and the cabs remained intact. The fuel tanks were left in place with instructions "not to fuel" written on them. Under normal operation, each road slug was semipermanently coupled to a GP40-2 set up with control equipment.

On June 17, 2004, CSX operated an office car special to Chicago on the former Chicago & Eastern Illinois. This view was made on the southward return trip at Cayuga, Indiana. In 1999, CSX acquired two Amtrak F40PHs for office car service. Amtrak 390 became CSX 9992 and 395 became CSX 9993. The old F40PHs had been rendered surplus by Amtrak with the delivery of large numbers of new GE Genesis locomotives. *Brian Solomon*

In the mid-1990s, CSX assigned a number of older locomotives to maintenance of way service and painted them a distinctive safety orange livery. On September 24, 1997, CSX GP40 9728 passes a Hyrail truck on the east slope of Sand Patch at Mance, Pennsylvania. *Brian Solomon*

Retirements

Modern high-horsepower diesels dominate today's CSX fleet. Yet numerous older models such as GP38s, GP40-2s, and B36-7s remain. Over time their ranks are being thinned out. Since 1980, CSX has retired many locomotives that it inherited from its predecessors and has purged a number of classes from its ranks.

By the mid-1980s, most of L&N's Alcos, and Seaboard's antiques, had been retired. In 1990, CSX listed 3,164 locomotives. By this time, most of the 1950s-era GP7s and GP9s had been retired except for the rebuilt GP16 fleet. The remaining GP16s were retired en masse at the end of 1992. Likewise, its once sizeable fleet of six-motor GE Universal line was down to just one serviceable unit, number

7256. Another U30C, 7258, survived another couple of years at the Huntington, West Virginia, shop as a test unit. A few four-motor Universal line locomotives survived through the 1990s, but all were gone by 2002. CSX's former Clinchfield F units were retired in the mid-1990s. The first to go was No. 119, which was retired in October following a main generator failure. All four F units were preserved.

CSX's Pumpkin Patch

In the mid-1990s, CSX reassigned several dozen older four-motor locomotives to maintenance of way (MOW) service. These were assigned new numbers, the 9500 series for General Electric and the 9600 and 9700 series for GM's Electro-Motive Division. To distinguish these locomotives from those in general service, MOW locomotives were

On a bright sunny day, CSX F7A 116 and F7B 117 are back on home rails as they lead the company inspection train at Rocky, North Carolina. Rocky is the siding location on former Clinchfield's famous loops in western North Carolina near Spruce Pine. The train is a rolling meeting room for Tennessee Eastman Chemical Co., a large CSX shipper. CSX 116 was built in December 1948 as Clinchfield F3A 800 and upgraded to F7A specifications in 1952. The differences between F3s and F7s were largely electrical. The F7 used substantially more robust traction motors and had many other improvements. Both F3s and F7s were rated at 1,500 horsepower. *Doug Koontz*

painted a bright shade of orange, similar to the color used on industry safety vests. Amtrak had painted some of its maintenance locomotives a similar shade. In both situations, the locomotives attained the color-logic nickname of "pumpkins." Among the pumpkins were 8 U18Bs, 6 U23Bs, 10 GP38s, and 17 GP40s. Most of these were close to retirement age.

Leased Fleet

In 2002, CSX had more than 3,400 locomotives. To keep its trains moving in recent years, CSX has regularly leased road locomotives from a variety of sources. In addition, run-through arrangements are very common, and it is normal to find locomotives from most major American railroads operating in daily service on CSX rails.

Monsoon on the Monon. Southward Q643 passes Linden, Indiana, during a July 2000 downpour. Train Q643 runs from Chicago's Barr Yard to Avon Yard near Indianapolis, and uses a portion of the former Monon in western Indiana. Following the Conrail split, CSX designated this portion of the old Monon as its Lafayette Subdivision, Great Lakes Division, Western Region. *Pete Ruesch*

CHAPTER FOUR

CSX OPERATIONS

Train Symbols

In railroad operations a "train" is a service and not specific equipment. A cut of cars sitting in a yard, or locomotives resting at terminal, do not necessarily qualify as a train. Every train operating on CSX carries a distinct symbol consisting of a letter followed by a three-digit number. When CSX dispatches a train, it is the service, represented by a train symbol, that qualifies as the train. During the course of its run, an individual train may change locomotives and switch out its consist.

Two CSX AC4400CWs lead an empty grain train G837 west toward the eastern continental divide on the former C&O Alleghany Subdivision on the fill at Jerrys Run, Virginia, on March 23, 2002. A massive fill of more than 1.5 million cubic yards of rock was required to bridge the large ravine formed by the small creek called Jerrys Run between Lewis Mountain and Brushy Mountain. This portion of the former C&O mainline was once double track, but reduced to single track between OX cabin and East Alleghany, Virginia. *T. S. Hoover*

CSXT's Grain Express insignia is displayed on the side of a covered hopper. *Bradley McClelland*

A locomotive that leads today's Q116 intermodal schedule may be assigned to move a set of empty hoppers tomorrow, and be sent to the shop the next day. The locomotive is not the Q116, it simply hauls it.

In current CSX symboling parlance, through trains with even-numbered symbols indicate eastward and northward schedules, and odd-numbered symbols indicate westward or southward schedules. Regularly scheduled intermodal, merchandise, and automotive trains are given "Q" symbols. Until 1997, many through schedules used "R" symbols, but these were dropped in favor of the "Q" symbols that were first used in 1992. ("Q" has the connotation of "quality"—a popular catchphrase of 1990s-era operations philosophy.) A variety of other letter prefixes are also used depending on the type of service. Some trains operating on alternative schedules

The former Baltimore & Ohio mainline over Sand Patch is a relatively busy double-track route. At 10:50 a.m. on October 28, 1992, the eastward R346 met the westward R135 intermodal train at the west portal of the Falls Cut Tunnel. B&O built the tunnel to ease the original alignment, which can be seen just above the R135. *Brian Solomon*

A 53-foot CSXI container rolls eastward through the snow at Warren, Massachusetts, on CSX Q116 in February 2003. *Brian Solomon*

To serve the intensive consumer market of the New York metro area, CSX runs a fleet of priority intermodal trains with former New York Central lines acquired from Conrail. CSX Q169 is scheduled to operate from North Bergen, New Jersey, to Willow Springs, Illinois, Tuesday through Saturday. It is seen on June 8, 2001, winding up the River Line at Milepost 44 north of the Bear Mountain Bridge near Fort Montgomery, New York. *Tim Doherty*

one or two days a week use "L" symbols. Trains in the Q100 series are intermodal schedules; Q200s are automotive; Q300s are east-west merchandise schedules; Q400s are north-south merchandise schedules in the eastern part of the system; Q500s are north-south merchandise schedules in the western part of the system; and Q600s are used for trains that cross corridors, such as those operating diagonally across the system between terminals.

Unit trains moving coal, ore, or grain do not necessarily operate on daily schedules and have their own letter prefixes. Unit coal trains may use "N," "T," "U," and "V" prefixes, and empty coal trains are assigned an "E" prefix. Grain trains use a "G" prefix, while most other unit commodity trains operate with a "K" prefix. Local trains, work trains, detours, and passenger trains all use specific prefixes.

Intermodal

CSX Transportation's subsidiary, CSX Intermodal, is one of the largest intermodal carriers in the United States. It was formed in 1987 and combined intermodal business operations of CSX Transportation and the recently acquired Sea-Land container company. Although CSX divested Sea-Land in 1999, CSXI remains a major intermodal player across the United States. CSX's predecessor railroads initiated intermodal trailer on flatcar (TOFC) operations in the 1950s. Intermodal traffic grew rapidly following the passage of the Staggers Act. By the late 1980s, intermodal growth was driving railroad traffic, and new technologies fueled intermodal growth. In 1987, CSX experimented with RoadRailer service—a concept first envisioned by C&O in the 1950s. For about a year CSX moved General Motors autoparts in RoadRailer trailers between Detroit and Atlanta. CSX abandoned the RoadRailer concept and embraced other new technology, especially double-stack container equipment for intermodal movements.

During the 1980s and early 1990s, CSX moved to increase clearances on its lines to

allow more extensive operation of double-stack container trains. By the mid-1990s, the South became the last major region in the United States to benefit from double-stack service. In 1993 and 1994, CSX increased clearances to 20 feet, 2 inches on its New Orleans–Atlanta, New Orleans–Jacksonville, and Atlanta–Jacksonville routes. This removed most restrictions on stack traffic traveling to major southeastern destinations and opened up a host of new routes, including Memphis–Atlanta–Miami, to stack traffic. Prior to this improvement, CSX's intermodal business between Chicago and Florida had increased 30 percent during 1992, and it added a priority intermodal train on this corridor in March 1993.

Conrail's massive intermodal presence had made it an attractive merger partner. An example of Conrail's volume is in the early 1990s; Conrail was moving 800,000 intermodal loads annually from the New York metro area. On April 22, 1999, the *Journal of Commerce* quoted Dan Murphy, director of CSX intermodal corporate communications, "The very bedrock of this merger is intermodal." He further explained, "Intermodal is the fast-growing segment of the company." With its share of Conrail, CSX significantly increased its share of domestic rail-borne intermodal traffic. CSX has formed strategic links with other railroads. In 2001, CSX and BNSF improved their intermodal links between Texas and Ohio, and east-west Florida traffic moving through the Memphis gateway. To improve service to Mexico, CSXI went into a partnership with Union Pacific in 2003 for shipments to and from the southeastern United States.

Today, CSXI serves 48 domestic intermodal terminals, and many are along CSX's rail lines. It is not surprising that with the scope of CSXI's intermodal business container and TOFC traffic, it would be among the most intensive aspects of CSX's railroad operations. In 2004, CSX operated 75

The morning of October 25, 1993, dawned clear and bright. CSX's priority intermodal train R135 departed the yard at Cumberland shortly after sunrise. It is seen ascending Sand Patch near Falls Cut, Pennsylvania, on its way to Chicago. *Brian Solomon*

Above: In the late 1980s and early 1990s, one of the hottest intermodal trains on CSX was the service marketed as the *Orange Blossom Special*, taking its name from the famous Seaboard Air Line passenger train. On December 18, 1992, CSX R191 crosses the Susquehanna River at Havre de Grace, Maryland. This bridge was the work of B&O's Arthur W. Thompson who built it after 1910 to replace an earlier bridge. Originally a car ferry was used to float railroad cars across the river. *Brian Solomon*

Right: The Baltimore to Chicago intermodal freight R137 descends the west slope of Sand Patch near the Shoo Fly Tunnel on October 26, 1993. Leading the train are four former Seaboard System B36-7s. Baltimore & Ohio and Chessie System had assigned high-horsepower four-motor Electro-Motive Division locomotives to priority trains. During the CSX era, high-horsepower, four-motor GEs became common. Today, six-motor GEs are standard on these services. *Brian Solomon*

Above: On the morning of September 27, 1997, fog clings to the hills near the Cumberland Narrows as CSX's former B&O yard in Cumberland, Maryland, goes about its business of sorting freight cars and assembling and taking apart trains. It has long been a nerve center on the B&O and is conveniently located east of the junction between its busy Chicago and St. Louis mainlines. Cumberland still serves a vital function for CSX. *Brian Solomon*

Left: CSX's yard in Cumberland, Maryland, is among its most important facilities in the eastern United States. It was substantially rebuilt, expanded, and modernized by B&O in the early 1960s. *Brian Solomon*

Chicago is America's busiest and most important railroad junction. CSX's most important Chicago facility is Barr Yard off Halsted Street, east of Blue Island. This busy facility was photographed at sunset in May 1996. Here interchanged cars are sorted before departing eastward on CSX. *William M. Beecher Jr*

The locomotive facility at CSX's Barr Yard on Chicago's south side on August 28, 1994. *Brian Solomon*

Above: Deep in the Ohio River valley, Cincinnati developed as a major transportation center in the east-central section of the United States. Before 1967, seven different railroads served Cincinnati. By the 1980s there were just three: CSX, Conrail, and Norfolk Southern. CSX lines into the Queen City includes former B&O, C&O, and L&N routes. At one time all three had several yards within the Cincinnati area. During the late 1970s, plans were made to consolidate older yards into Queensgate Yard. This photo was made on June 15, 1996. *Bradley McClelland*

Left: The exit sign at Cincinnati's Queensgate Yard promotes railroad safety. Queensgate Yard never sleeps. It processes between 1,900 and 2,400 cars in a 24-hour period. It takes an average of 16 hours to process and assemble freight cars. This facility serves as a primary north-south hub in originating 23 daily trains. It handles about 45 percent of all finished automobiles on the CSX system. In a given 24 hours, anywhere from 60 to 70 trains originate at or pass though Queensgate Yard. *Bradley McClelland*

The former B&O yard at New Castle, Pennsylvania, serves Pittsburgh-area traffic. The large yard was originally built during the administration of Leonor F. Loree in the early years of the twentieth century. It is situated just west of the junction between the former Pittsburgh & Lake Erie water level route through Pittsburgh and the B&O's grade-intensive Pittsburgh & Western mainline. Long before CSX acquired the P&LE route, B&O routed traffic via the P&LE east of New Castle. ***Brian Solomon***

Q100-series intermodal trains on expedited schedules five to seven days a week. Dozens more trains were operated on alternate days, or on an as-needed basis, or as extra sections of regularly scheduled trains. In 2000, CSX intermodal trains traveled at an average of 30 miles per hour, the highest average speed of any freight moving on the railroad.

CSX's most intensive intermodal routes are on former New York Central lines inherited from Conrail. Over the route of the famed *Twentieth Century Limited,* CSX operates dozens of daily intermodal trains. But unlike the *Twentieth Century Limited,* CSX's Chicago-bound traffic uses the B&O to reach Chicago west of Cleveland. Its fastest runs between Little Ferry, New Jersey (across the Hudson from New York City), and Chicago, take just a little more than 20 hours, point to point. More typical services on this route take 23 hours or more.

Automotive Traffic

CSX consolidated its automotive train symbols under the 200 series in December 1995. In 2004, the vast majority of new automotive shipments were moved in dedicated Q200-series trains. Automobiles and small trucks are carried in specialized freight cars called multilevels. Each consists of two or three levels, depending on the size of the vehicles transported. Tri-levels are commonly used for passenger cars. When this type of specialized freight car was developed, they were open to the air. Today they are fully enclosed with galvanized steel sheets to prevent theft and vandalism. In the 1980s, clearance improvement programs allowed the operation of covered trilevels, which were significantly taller than most traditional freight cars. Multilevel loading is performed from car ends. They are easily loaded and unloaded at terminals by driving automobiles along the length of the cars. A dedicated CSX multilevel train has a uniform appearance that looks like a mile-long, yellow-faced snake as it rolls along on welded rail. Their uniformity and size are especially impressive when passing at speed. It is as if block after block of windowless two-story buildings are gliding past you.

CSX's Q200-series trains typically operate on tight schedules to ensure prompt delivery of new automobiles and timely return of empty multilevels. The typical CSX multilevel travels at an average speed of 21 miles per hour. In 2004, CSX had more than 50 daily scheduled Q200-series trains operating across its system. In addition to daily trains, another 25 or so trains operate on less than daily schedules.

With the June 1999 assumption of Conrail operations, CSX obtained a significantly larger share of auto-traffic because Conrail's former New York Central Water Level Route had long been a major artery for this business. According to *Jane's World Railways,* Conrail moved 20 percent of all finished automotive vehicles in the United States and was the largest carrier of automotive parts in 1994. At that time, Conrail served 23 assembly plants and 59 automotive component factories. The

With the split of Conrail, CSX greatly expanded its automotive traffic. Dedicated multilevel trains use the former New York Central Water Level Route to reach central distribution points in New York, New Jersey, and Massachusetts. In April 2001, a DASH 8-40C leads a westward empty multilevel train on the Selkirk Branch at Guilderland, New York, a few miles west of the former New York Central Selkirk Yard. *Brian Solomon*

On the evening of October 28, 1992, an empty westward CSX auto carrier train consisting of multilevel auto carriers crests the summit at Sand Patch. On the former B&O, automotive traffic is largely eastbound. *Brian Solomon*

In its contemporary system of train symbol organization, CSX assigned automotive carrying trains Q200-series symbols to distinguish them from other types of traffic. In June 2004, CSX Q244 heads northward on the former C&EI at Bismarck, north of Dansville, Illinois. In 2004, CSX Q244 was listed as a daily train between Louisville, Kentucky, and Gibson, Indiana, via Evansville. *Brian Solomon*

Along the former Monon Chicago to Louisville mainline, northward train R594 (Louisville to St. Louis) leans into the curve at Borden, Indiana, on October 27, 1994. The middle portion of the former Monon mainline between Bloomington and Bedford was abandoned in March 1993. In the summer of 1994, CSX changed the name of the southern section of the former Monon to the Hoosier Subdivision. In addition to CSX traffic, CP Rail operates via trackage rights on this line. *John Leopard*

A modern defect detection car negotiates street trackage in Clearwater, Florida, on the line to St. Petersburg. The modern Gage Restraint Measurement System (GRMS) evaluates track conditions, tie replacement, and the effectiveness of track maintenance programs. This is among the most advanced pieces of track analyzing equipment in CSX's fleet. *Marshall W. Beecher*

Florida phosphate traffic has long been a staple of CSX and its predecessors. By the 1960s, the railroads faced growing competition from trucks for this lucrative traffic, but retained the business by lowering their rates. CSX maintains a complex network of branchlines on the Bone Valley Subdivision near Tampa to serve phosphate industries. In March 1999, a CSX phosphate local shoves back into the former SAL Mulberry Yard. Although it is rare system-wide, cabooses are still used here to aid in reverse moves. *Marshall W. Beecher*

largest concentration of automotive factories was in northern Ohio and southern Michigan. Conrail had a fleet of approximately 5,500 multilevel auto racks to handle finished automotive traffic. Loaded multilevels cannot be sorted at hump yards because the humping process risks damage to new cars, so they are flat-switched. One of Conrail's primary multilevel sorting facilities was Collinwood Yard near Cleveland. With the Conrail acquisition, CSX obtained a portion of its automotive traffic. Collinwood is now an important CSX facility for eastward loaded multilevel trains. Since NS now operates the New York Central Water Level Route west of Cleveland, CSX multilevel trains follow the B&O/New York Central Big Four routing via Greenwich and Willard. CSX Q290 is an example. It is scheduled to operate daily from Detroit to Cleveland on a C-shaped route by way of Walbridge, near Toledo, Fostoria, and Willard, Ohio. The Q290's schedule has it departing Detroit in the early morning and arriving in Cleveland 12 to 14 hours later.

On December 12, 1992, the Q649 negotiates a curved bridge on former Louisville & Nashville trackage across the Ohio River flood plain south of Evansville, Indiana. *Scott Muskopf*

Coal

Historically coal was the lifeblood of many CSX predecessor lines. The C&O, L&N, and Clinchfield thrived on the flow of bituminous coal. Coal provided B&O the revenue needed to build its lines over the mountains, and in later years kept the line afloat when all else in the industry seemed to be in decline. In the *History of the Louisville & Nashville Railroad,* Maury Klein wrote that in 1970 the railroad moved 48,146,273 tons of coal, representing 666,861 carloads.

Against a stormy summer sky, CSX SD40-2 8879 with Q642 is on the siding at Linden, Indiana, in July 2001. The pending storm would ultimately dump 4 inches of rain. Linden is the most significant siding between Indianapolis and Lafayette. CSX's Q642 is a merchandise train that operates from Avon Yard at Indianapolis to Chicago's Barr Yard, running via the Crawfordsville branch at North Hunt westward to Crawfordsville, and from there northward on the old Monon via Lafayette. ***Ryan Krengel***

Coal remains CSX's heaviest traffic commodity. In 2000, CSX moved 1,660,000 carloads of coal, which represented 25 percent of the railroad's revenue. In 2002, coal represented 41.5 percent of tonnage originated by

CSX. The scope of CSX's coal operations is staggering. In the Appalachian coal fields of Virginia, West Virginia, and Kentucky, where the largest portion of its coal originates on the former B&O, C&O, Clinchfield, and L&N lines, CSX maintains complex myriads of lines that serve mines, small and large. CSX reported that it served more than 127 active coal mines in 2001. As this book was being written, CSX reported that for the week ending November 26, 2004, it had operated 1,339 coal trains, which was just less than the six-week average of 1,481 weekly trains. CSX had a daily average 16,819 coal loads on its rails.

Where does all the coal go? Traditionally, coal was used for heating homes, powering heavy industry, steel making, and electrical generation. In 1970, Klein explains that 13 percent of L&N's coal went for export, 17 percent was used as industrial coke, 17 percent was used for other industry, and 53 percent was used for commercial electrical generation. Today, coal-fired power stations are among CSX's biggest customers. In 2001, CSX provided service to 105 electrical generating stations. CSX moves coal to waterfront piers for transloading to ships. It exports coal from piers at Baltimore; Newport News, Virginia; and Mobile, Alabama. After a decade of slack and declining coal export, CSX's export coal had rebounded in 2004. CSX reported that export shipments had increased 65 to 70 percent (by volume) over 2003. A significant portion of this renewed traffic comes from metallurgical coal used in steel making. The booming Chinese economy is one of the primary markets for export metallurgical coal.

Today the average speed of a CSX loaded coal train is 15 to 16 miles per hour. The nature of profitable coal transport depends on volume, not speed. Railroads are ideal transporters of coal because they can efficiently and relatively inexpensively move trains weighing up to 21,000 tons. Since coal is not perishable and can be consistently mined from the ground and consumed at predictable rates, it is not necessary to transport it quickly. Greater speed requires greater energy, and greater energy increases the cost of transport. Balancing factors in the equation of moving coal are labor costs, the value of hoppers and locomotives, and line capacity. The utilization of these resources must be weighed against fuel consumption. Saving fuel costs is only valid up to a point. If trains move too slowly, these other considerations will incur a greater cost than fuel. One of the challenges in shipping coal over CSX is the difficult terrain from which coal is mined. Much of CSX's coal comes from the mountains, which means that coal often has to ascend steep grades to get to where it is needed. This is one reason that C&O and Clinchfield were ideal coal routes because while they had traversed the Appalachians, they had relatively low grade profiles and were more cost-effective lines for moving coal trains.

C&O Coal

Historically, C&O was a coal conveyor belt and moved rivers of coal east to the Virginia tidewater at Newport News, along to transloading facilities on Lake Erie near Toledo, Ohio. Coal was gathered from mines on C&O's network of branches and transported for sorting and classified at centralized yards at Russell, Kentucky, and Huntington, West Virginia. Russell was the largest yard on C&O and remains an important facility on modern CSX. Its hump yard dated to 1918. In 1944, S. Kip Farrington Jr. reported in his book, *Railroads at War,* that Russell classified more than 75 percent of all the coal that originated on C&O rails. Historically, as many as 14,538 coal hoppers were processed daily at Russell. Farrington explains that loaded trains from the coal fields operated directly to Russell, where hoppers were weighed, classified, routed, and assembled into trains. Westward coal trains were routed to Toledo (via Columbus) or to Cincinnati for forwarding to western and southern connections. Fascinated by the

CSXT AC4400CW 295 exits the Red Rock Tunnel with empty hopper train E651 west (Newport News to Hinton) on the east slope of the grade to the summit of the Blue Ridge near Afton, Virginia, on the former C&O North Mountain Subdivision on March 10, 2003. The 13-mile ascent of the east slope of the Blue Ridge, designed by Claudius Crozet during the original expansion of the C&O to the west, required four tunnels, including the Blue Ridge Tunnel near the summit. The route has since been improved several times to reduce grade and curvature, but the unlined Red Rock Tunnel remains as originally constructed. *T. S. Hoover*

A DASH 8-40C leads northward CMIX coal loads across the Kentucky River at Yerkey, Kentucky, on the EK Subdivision of the old Louisville & Nashville in December 1994. It was loaded at the Consolidated Minerals Leatherwood prep plant south of Hazard. (CMIX is the reporting mark used by Consolidated Minerals hoppers.) At Jackson, Kentucky, 20 miles ahead, helpers will tie on the rear to push this train up the Elkatawa hill. Coal was the lifeblood of the old L&N, and it remains an important source of traffic for CSX on former L&N routes. *William M. Beecher Jr.*

tides of C&O coal, Farrington also wrote about it in *Railroads from the Head End,* where he cites a figure of 15,654,717 tons were moved annually via the Presque Isle docks for transloading into Lake Erie ships. This represented an astounding 265,231 loaded hoppers—or an average of 727 hoppers a day. Each of these cars worked their way over C&O rails in 160-car, 13,500-ton trains behind the railroad's massive class T-1 2-10-4 Texas types, clattering across the multiple diamond crossings at Marion and Fostoria on their lake-bound trip.

This was just a portion of the flood of coal moving over wartime C&O, which also interchanged coal trains with the Erie Railroad at Marion, Ohio; the Nickel Plate at Fostoria, Ohio; the Pennsylvania Railroad at Columbus; and New York Central's Big Four route. A portion of westward coal continued to Chicago over C&O's own line via Cincinnati. Today, a typical CSX unit train bound for the coal pier facility at Toledo is symbol U918, which loads at A.T. Massey Company's Liberty tipple on the Coal River Subdivision. After loading, U918 travels to the connection with the former C&O mainline at St. Albans, West Virginia; U918 travels west over the former

C&O via Russell, Kentucky, and Columbus, Ohio, to Toledo, Ohio. Instead of a massive T-1, today AC4400CWs do the work.

Eastward coal traverses the New River Gorge, ascends Alleghany Summit via White Sulphur Springs, Clifton Forge, and then follows the C&O low grade line along the James River to Richmond, then on to the vast dockside facilities at Newport News. In 1942, the yards held capacity for 10,300 coal hoppers.

A southward loaded coal train rolls down the former Atlantic Coast Line mainline at Folkston, Georgia, on February 17, 2001. The ACL route was once largely a directional double-track line between Richmond, Virginia, and Jacksonville, Florida. Today much of the route has been reduced to a single main operated by CTC. This section is still double track, with a maximum track speed of 79 miles per hour for passenger trains, and 70 miles per hour for intermodal freight. The line diverging on the left is the Jessup Subdivision, which heads toward Waycross, Georgia, the location of a large CSX yard. *Don Marson*

As with westward coal trains, the standard length in the steam era for eastward trains was 160 cars. The terminal was organized so the receiving yard could accommodate 10 entire coal trains at once. In 1942, Farrington reported that 4.3 million tons of coal were dumped into ships at Newport News. This was a low figure because of the German U-boat blockade. At that time the yearly record was more than 10 million tons of coal. From Newport News, coal was moved in barges up the coast for consumption in the Northeast, as well as sent overseas in ships. Today, most of the coal moving via Newport News is exported. CSX T712 is a typical modern unit coal train operating to the coal pier in Newport News, Virginia. Typically, this train consists of CSX-owned hoppers or gondolas. Like the U918, described earlier, T712 is loaded at A.T. Massey Company's Liberty tipple on the Coal River Subdivision. From the connection

A road slug set consisting of a former GP30 leading and a GP40 operate a mine run hauling coal loads at North Edjouet, Kentucky, in May 1998. This run will terminate at North Hazard, Kentucky, one of several principal coal gathering yards on the former L&N. CSX operates a maze of coal lines throughout central Appalachia. ***W. M. Beecher Jr.***

Coal trains operate across the CSX system; some to reach ports for export, others for interchange, and many for use at electrical power stations. Most CSX coal is moved in dedicated unit trains. This empty unit coal train waits for a crew near South Birch, Michigan, on the former Pere Marquette on September 13, 2000. *Brian Solomon*

with the former C&O mainline at St. Albans, West Virginia, T712 travels east the length of the former C&O to the Atlantic Ocean. A single manned AC4400CW rear-end helper locomotive is required to assist large coal trains east over the Alleghany summit. Coal trains on the C&O are some of the heaviest on CSX. The relatively easy grade profile and gentle curvature of the C&O route allows for the operation of 19,000-ton trains carrying 150 modern cars.

At one time, railroads such as C&O provided the bulk of coal hoppers moving over their lines. Today it is a common practice for utility customers to provide their own hopper cars and have them built to specifications tailored to their requirements. CSX U428 loads at Premier Elkhorn Coal in Myra, Kentucky, on the former C&O, which is now in CSX's Big Sandy Rate district and used by an electrical generating station near Columbia, South Carolina. Myra is a modern coal facility

The original B&O mainline went west from Cumberland, Maryland, to Keyser, West Virginia, and from there it crossed the spine of the Alleghenies and climbed the famous Seventeen Mile Grade to the summit at Altamont, Maryland. Since the St. Louis route west of Clarksburg, West Virginia, was severed in 1985, the old B&O West End has largely served as a coal funnel. However, a pair of mixed freights still plies the line daily. On October 26, 1991, CSX R317 ascends the Seventeen Mile Grade at milepost 216 near the Hitchcock Tunnel. *Brian Solomon*

designed to load unit coal trains quickly. To reach its destination, U428 passes the old C&O terminal at Shelby, Kentucky, then traverses the length of the former Clinchfield Railroad, now operated as CSX's KP and BR Subdivisions, which runs from Elkhorn City, Kentucky, to Spartanburg, South Carolina. For this journey, a pair of AC4400CWs are used in the lead, while manned rear-end helpers are required to assist on the Clinchfield Grades over the Alleghany and Blue Ridge summits.

B&O Coal

Coal originating on the former B&O is shipped eastward for both utility customers in the Mid-Atlantic region and to the port of Baltimore for export. CSX unit coal train T861 is known on the Mountain Subdivision (what CSX calls the old B&O West End) as the Whitetail from the mine where it's loaded. This is a typical unit train of steam coal crossing the former B&O and consists of 80 loaded hoppers weighing 10,500 tons. Unlike trains on the C&O that can weigh almost twice as much, unit trains moving over the old B&O West End are limited because of the line's severe grades and curvature. After leaving Coastal Coal's new Whitetail tipple near Newburg, West Virginia, T861 crosses the Newburg, Cheat River, Cranberry, and Seventeen Mile Grades of the Mountain Subdivision to

CSX AC4400CW 295 leads empty hopper train E651 (Newport News to Hinton) across the former Southern Railway mainline at JC cabin in Charlottesville, Virginia, on CSX's North Mountain Subdivision on March 10, 2003. This former C&O mainline from Richmond to Clifton Forge was primarily used for passenger and manifest trains. CSX has used the North Mountain Subdivision to return empty trains west to avoid the busy river-grade James River Subdivision required for heavy loaded eastbound trains. In 2004, CSX arranged to lease this line to the Buckingham Branch Railroad. *T. S. Hoover*

Two AC4400CWs with eastbound coal train N606-09 exit the east portal of the Big Bend Tunnel at Talcott, West Virginia, on the Alleghany Subdivision on March 10, 2001. Col. R. H. Talcott was the resident engineer during the construction of the original tunnel (a now-abandoned bore parallel to the Great Bend Tunnel). C&O constructed the Big Bend Tunnel to cut off a large loop (or Great Bend) in the Greenbrier River. At full load, locomotives struggle to avoid their own heat exhaust in the 6,192-foot-long bore. The challenge of this location led CSX to use it for new locomotive tunnel testing in 2004. *T. S. Hoover*

Cumberland. Climbing the Cranberry Grade will require four AC4400CWs, two on the front and a two-unit manned helper on the rear. The descent of the Seventeen Mile Grade is limited to 10 miles per hour after a fatal accident in 2000. East of Cumberland, T861 follows the former B&O mainline east through Harpers Ferry and Brunswick, to reach a utility at Dickerson, Maryland.

Helpers

The grade-intensive profiles of many CSX routes require lots of power to move trains. Operating heavy coal trains and long manifests trains over very curvy and steep Appalachian crossings often requires helpers—extra locomotives assigned in graded territory. Helpers allow for a more efficient use of motive power by concentrating power where it is needed. Rather than assigning three AC4400CWs to each train ascending a stiff grade and leaving them on for the full length of the run, including across less-demanding territory, CSX may assign just two lead units and use a helper on just the steepest sections. A single helper can assist several trains during the course of a day. CSX has more manned helper operations than any

A unit coal train heads eastward through Richmond, Virginia, toward Fulton Yard, and ultimately to Newport News for export. The flow of eastward coal trains over the C&O, which had subsided considerably in recent years, began to rebound in 2004 as a result of changes in the export coal market. *Brian Solomon*

An empty unit coal train departs CSX's Fulton Yard in Richmond, Virginia, on February 15, 2004. Fulton, like coal traffic on the old C&O, is now a shadow of its former greatness. *Brian Solomon*

A coal train bound for a Florida utility exits the Pool Point Tunnel and crosses the Russell Fork of the Big Sandy River at Pool Point, Kentucky, on CSX's KP Subdivision on November 2, 2002. This location, on the northern end of the Elkhorn Extension of the former Clinchfield Railroad near Elkhorn City, is the foot of the ruling grade against southbound coal. Rear-end helpers are required from Shelby to the summit at Trammel, Virginia. *T. S. Hoover*

other North American railroad. Unlike western railroads, CSX has shied away from the use of unmanned radio-control helpers, known in the industry as distributed power units (DPUs). According to Author Jay Potter, CSX operates manned helpers on 23 subdivisions, and this accounts for 30 sections of graded line. On about half of these lines, just a single 3,000-horsepower locomotive is needed, and on the other half, two or three units are routinely needed to get trains over the road.

Signaling

Kenneth C. Dufford Transportation Center

In 1988, CSX was the first of the large American railroads to implement a systemwide centralized operations center. The Kenneth C. Dufford Transportation Center is located in Jacksonville, Florida, and housed CSX dispatchers that directed operations across its system. At an estimated cost of $23 million, Union Switch & Signal provided the

On March 23, 2004, AC4400CW 433 leads northbound empty hopper train N389-15 on the former Clinchfield Railroad at Spruce Pine, North Carolina. This portion of the former Clinchfield south of Erwin, Tennessee, is CSX's BR (standing for Blue Ridge) Subdivision. During the previous 25 miles, this northbound train climbed to the summit of the Blue Ridge via the Clinchfield loops. *T. S. Hoover*

This Cumberland Coal Business Unit sign is on the old B&O office building in Grafton, West Virginia. The Cumberland Coal unit covered coal services on the old B&O. In the 1990s, CSX hoped to improve its customer focus by giving different areas of its business specialized attention. The unit coal trains looked the same. *Brian Solomon*

state-of-the-art, centralized, computer-aided dispatching center. This replaced a host of existing regional dispatching centers. As originally planned, it was to house 35 dispatching desks and employ approximately 500 people. This system lost its system-wide significance with the inclusion of former Conrail lines in June 1999, as Conrail lines continued to be dispatched from existing regional dispatching centers, including those at Selkirk, New York, and Indianapolis, Indiana. CSX also maintained a separate dispatching center at Calumet City, Illinois, for control of B&OCT trackage in Chicago. This had been controlled from the Belt Railway of Chicago's office until early 1999. In 2003, CSX hired US&S to upgrade its Jacksonville dispatching center with a more modern system.

Baltimore & Ohio Towers

B&O had an early interest in directing train operation strictly by signal indication. In 1925, Stanton Ennes, B&O's former General Manager of its Lines East, wrote in *Railway Signaling,* "Running trains by signal indication instead of train orders, substituting signal indication for train order, presents the biggest opportunity for reducing costs offered the railroads in years." With the development of Centralized Traffic Control (CTC) in the late 1920s, B&O was among the first to install CTC and use it to improve capacity on its single-track bottleneck between Grafton

For a few months in 1988, CSX assigned its executive Fs to premier RoadRailer service between Detroit and Atlanta. On June 26, 1988, former Clinchfield FP7 118 and F7B 119 lead the southward RoadRailer, train R211, at Robbins Street in Covington, Kentucky. *Bradley McClelland*

A southward CSX freight plies former Monon trackage running through the streets of New Albany, Indiana, on February 6, 1994. New Albany is across the Ohio River from Louisville, Kentucky, the Monon's southern terminus. Monon was absorbed by CSX predecessor Louisville & Nashville in 1971. The lead locomotive, GP40-2 No. 6401, wears an interim paint livery featuring a gray body and cab, with a bright yellow nose. *Scott Muskopf*

Looking west from M&K Junction toward Rowlesburg, West Virginia, CSX's Mountain Subdivision, the old B&O West End. A set of light helpers drifts down toward the yard. A classic B&O color position light signal displays "stop and proceed." *Brian Solomon*

An old Union Switch & Signal color light signal on the former Atlantic Coast Line mainline. This signal is set up to allow for block protection in either direction on either track of a double-track mainline segment. After World War II, ACL made a large investment in modern signaling, respacing block signals to allow for faster operation, replacing upper-quadrant semaphores with less-maintenance-intensive color lights, and installing hundreds of miles of CTC. *Brian Solomon*

Five minutes after sunset on April 6, 1997, the crescendo of a freight train rumbling over uneven jointed rail and a blast from the air horn for the county road culminates with CSX R591 passing this aged semaphore. This signal, located 2 miles north of the former Greencastle, Indiana, was installed in 1913 as part of a then state-of-art absolute permissive block (APB) system on the Monon. It was originally the approach signal for the north end of Greencastle siding until the signals from that location south to Bedford were removed in 1992 with the opening of the Conrail connection at Greencastle. *Eric Powell*

A modern color light signal protects the diamond crossing on the former Seaboard Air Line at Hamlet, North Carolina. *Brian Solomon*

Local freight CSX J768 splits the classic Monon semaphores at milepost 133.2 in South Romney, Indiana, on December 27, 2001. This former Conrail DASH 8-40B and CSX DASH 8-40CW have 70 cars in tow. The section of the former Monon mainline between Lafayette and Crawfordsville still hosts as many as 10 trains a day. These vintage General Railway Signal type 2A upper quadrant semaphores were state-of-the-art signaling back when the 2-8-2 Mikado-type was considered modern power. Today Type 2As provide a striking contrast to the high-horsepower diesel electrics CSX freights use. Time is running out and as of October 2004, several remaining Monon semaphores have been tagged with "do not repair" decals. *Eric Powell*

and Parkersburg, West Virginia. It also installed CTC on its heavily traveled line between Needmore Yard in North Dayton, Ohio, and Erie Junction near Lima, Ohio.

Despite its interest in using modern signaling to supplant train order operation, B&O was reluctant to embrace extensive pushbutton CTC installations on its busy double-track mainline network, unlike other CSX component railroads that invested heavily in modern CTC after World War II. Instead, it continued to rely on traditional manned signal towers at crucial points. In 1958, B&O had more than 240 active towers. Most of these had block operators who also operated switches and signals. The exact function of each tower varied depending on the demands of the specific location it served. Many B&O towers fit the classic stereotype of an elevated trackside structure with a gently sloped roof, but others were just small ground-level cabins or located inside passenger stations. Despite modernization and the consolidation of facilities, CSX continued to maintain traditional towers along much of its former B&O mainlines well into the 1990s. By 1995, less than 200 active towers were left in all of the United States, and a significant portion of these were on CSX's former B&O routes. As of this writing, a few old B&O towers remain in service.

Towers were traditionally identified by a one- or two-letter telegraph coding that dates from the time when tower operators communicated exclusively via Morse code. Letter coding identifications were unique within a

Above: CSX was the first American railroad to introduce a unified central dispatching center for its entire railroad. This modern facility is located in Jacksonville, Florida. The James River dispatcher, which controls former C&O lines in Virginia, observes the screens that tell him the condition of his railroad. He uses desktop computer controls to remotely set signals and line switches. He can communicate directly with train crews by radio. The displays that show his territory are color coded: red lines are occupied track, green lines are tracks that have signals lined for a train movement, and white lines are unoccupied track. *Doug Koontz*

Left: In October 1991, at Miller Tower, Cherry Run, West Virginia, CSX operator Jim Vargo discussed operations with the dispatcher in Jacksonville, Florida. Into the mid-1990s, numerous towers remained active on former B&O lines. *Brian Solomon*

An eastward CSX train of Coke Express hoppers passes a color position light signal at Curtis, Indiana, on January 2, 1995. This signal is unusual because it can display virtually all standard aspects in the traditional B&O rule book. The color position light uses white and lunar white dots to modify the basic red, yellow, and green aspects. The position and color of the modifying light is a crucial part of the aspect. The modifying light can be placed left, center and right, or top and bottom of the primary aspect that is displayed by the two colored lights in the circular portion of the signal head. *Brian Solomon*

given operating division, but not necessarily unique across the system. For example, both Hyndman Tower on B&O's Pittsburgh Division and Hardman Tower on the Cumberland Division carried the telegraph designation "Q." After CSX transferred dispatching functions to Jacksonville, tower letter codes were largely dropped.

Despite their technological obsolescence, B&O towers functioned well in the CSX era and continued to perform the duty for which they had been installed. A number of towers employed electro-mechanical plants that combined basic mechanical interlocking machinery with some electric controls. Typically on the B&O, these installations used mechanical interlocking mechanisms—often using the Saxby & Farmer patent—to prevent routing conflicts. Mechanical levers and pipeline rods moved switch lock and points, and signals (and possibly some distant switches) were operated electrically. B&O had routinely converted all-mechanical installations to electro-mechanical in conjunction with the switch from traditional three-position semaphores to its unique color position light (CPL) signals. In some situations, B&O combined the functions of two or more nearby towers at one location by using electrically controlled switches and signals for the more remote locations. This provided a safe yet economical signaling solution that in many instances performed adequately for decades. Not all towers date from the steam era. Modern B&O facilities used pushbutton installations with all-electric relay interlocking equipment. Economy, rather than technology, often dictated B&O's signaling solutions.

Towers were worked by operators, who took direction from the line's dispatcher and controlled the operation of switches and signals that govern the movements of trains. Home signals at towers are absolute, and like modern CTC home signals, authorize the movements of trains. The human presence in railroad signaling has a value that cannot be entirely supplanted by purely technological solutions. Having an experienced operator on-site can provide a level of safety and efficiency not possible with remote technology.

Tower Closings

Since 1987, CSX has closed most of its remaining towers and consolidated their functions to Jacksonville. The list of closures only tells part of the story. Line-side towers survived much longer on former B&O routes than on most other North American railways. The introduction of CTC systems in the 1920s gave railroads the ability to consolidate and close towers. On many railroads, towers survived at very busy junctions or at crossings with other company's tracks; but on B&O many towers survived at a multitude of places, including protection for mainline crossovers, at entrances to yards, and places where helpers were added (or removed) from trains. Surviving B&O towers provided a dramatic technological contrast. On CSX's Mountain Sub (B&O West End), where CSX has regularly assigned its most modern motive power, the roar of high-horsepower AC4400CWs and SD70MACs coexisted with the traditional sounds of mechanical interlocking. Here heavy coal trains led by modern diesels have passed the same interlocking towers that once governed the movements of B&O's legendary EM-1 articulated steam locomotives.

Among the closures are FN Tower at Patterson Creek, West Virginia, east of Cumberland, Maryland, in 1991. The December 1995 *CTC Board* reported that GK Tower at East Norwood, Ohio, closed in August 1995, and a month later NA Tower at Ivorydale, Ohio, was finished. Its UN Tower at the east of the former B&O New Castle, Pennsylvania, yard closed in November 1995.

On December 29, 1995, AM Tower at Altamont, Maryland, closed. Located a few hundred feet west of the summit of the Seventeen Mile Grade, 2,628 feet above sea level, AM Tower controlled a pair of crossovers where helpers were typically cut out of westbound trains. It had survived because of its strategic location at the top of one of the railroad's most difficult mountain grades. What makes the Seventeen Mile Grade especially tough is the long descent for heavily loaded coal trains. A few seconds of inattention on the part of the locomotive engineer or faulty brake equipment can result in a runaway train. In the steam era, B&O installed runaway tracks on the eastward mainline below Altamont at Strecker (HX) and Bond (BD). Both of the runaway tracks were removed in the diesel era. On January 30, 2000, more than four years after AM closed, CSX experienced one of its worse runaways in modern memory. Symbol V986-26, an 80-car eastward coal train, lost its brakes descending the Seventeen Mile Grade. It careened out of control and derailed near Piedmont, Maryland; one of the derailed hoppers crashed into a house and killed a sleeping child.

In July 1996, CSX closed Mexico Tower. This facility was located at the east end of CSX's Cumberland Yard, and dated from the modernization of the yard in 1960. Its telegraph symbol was "M" for Mexico, the name taken from a nearby farm. CSX closed Cumberland's other surviving tower, ND Tower at Viaduct Junction, in January 1997 after nearly

95 years of continuous service. In recent years this tower controlled the important junction (named for the nearby arched viaduct) between the old B&O West End and the mainline to Pittsburgh and Chicago. According to an article in the February 1997 issue of *The Bull Sheet*, when it was built, ND Tower also controlled a crossing with the Cumberland & Pennsylvania.

One of the more complex towers that CSX closed was 75th Street Tower in Chicago, which was closed after Thanksgiving in 1997. According to *The Home Signal,* this tower housed a 132-lever Saxby & Farmer interlocking machine and had once controlled crossings of the B&OCT with the Belt Railway of Chicago; Norfolk Southern's former Wabash; and, until the 1980s, Conrail's former Pennsylvania Panhandle route that ran parallel to B&O. The tower was closed as part of general reconfiguration of the trackage at this important junction.

Not all towers have closed simply because technology superceded them. On May 6, 1987, a CSX freight derailed at speed and demolished CF Tower at Confluence, Pennsylvania. The operator perished in the accident. CSX replaced the tower with a remote CTC installation.

B&O Color Position Light Signals

Certainly the most distinctive, and by far the most unusual variety of signal hardware on CSX lines is the color position light (CPL), which is used primarily on former B&O lines. This type of signal was developed for B&O by Frank Paternall after World War I. He had emigrated to America from England in 1885, had worked with signaling in Britain, and served as an employee of Union Switch & Signal before he went to work for B&O in 1891. Paternall's CPL features a unique way of displaying aspects by combining the position and the color of lights in a simple recognizable pattern. The arrangement of the primary lights was designed to mimic the positions of a three-position upper quadrant semaphore blade, the most common style of signal in use on B&O at that time. The combination of light position and colors was designed to minimize the potential of a signal being misinterpreted. Furthermore, a single signal head is used to display all aspects in the rule book, unlike most other types of signal designs that often require two or more heads to display a full range of aspects. Using marker lights, the four basic aspects (clear, approach, restricting, and stop) are modified for speed signaling. The marker light can occupy any of six positions (top left, top center, top right, bottom left, bottom center, bottom right) or be unlit. The marker light uses either a yellow or lunar white, depending on its position. For normal route signals, "clear" is represented by a pair of green lights one above the other with a lunar white dot above; "approach" is a pair of yellow lights at a 45-degree angle from one another with a white light centered above them; a full "stop" is a pair of horizontal red lights on a signal without a number plate.

Among the benefits of the CPL system is that a dwarf signal is capable of displaying all the same aspects as a tall signal. Although the CPL system was originally designed to display just 14 aspects, a number of additional aspects were later developed. Over the years, B&O and its successors altered and adapted the aspects displayed by these signals. The August 1, 2001, *CSX Transportation Signal Aspect and Indication Rules* guide lists 22 different aspects displayed by CPL signals. By virtue of this style of signal, as many as 29 aspects are possible.

The CPL fell out of favor with CSX in the mid-1990s. The desire to simplify the number of aspects system-wide and standardize its signal hardware has led it to adopt the C&O arrangement of color lights at most new signal installations. As of this writing in 2004, CPLs have largely been replaced on the former B&O mainlines between Baltimore and Chicago, yet remain on many secondary former B&O routes.

In May 1998, at Shoals, Indiana, westward freight travels from Cincinnati to St. Louis on former B&O rails, which was CSX's Indiana Subdivision of its Chicago Division. In the distance, an old B&O color position light displays two red lights and mimics the position of a semaphore in the stop position and uses colored lights to reinforce this aspect. *Pete Ruesch*

C&O Color Lights

C&O was not as quick to adopt automatic signaling as some railroads. The earliest automatic block signals dated to the 1880s, and by late 1890, the electrically operated two-aspect, lower-quadrant semaphore had been perfected. C&O refrained from installing automatic block signaling until 1910, when it equipped its mainline between Newport News and Richmond, and between Clifton Forge and Cincinnati with electrically operated upper-quadrant semaphores. This type of signaling was generally used to increase capacity and improve protection of following movements, which is especially important on a conveyor belt operation like C&O where trains closely follow one another. In 1929, C&O was among the first lines to replace semaphores with color light signals, and by 1942, most of its mainlines were protected with color light automatic block signaling.

The typical C&O signal is a vertical three-light head. Like a common traffic light used for highway applications, each light on the signal head displays just one color—red, yellow, or green—and only one light at a time is lit. For this reason, two and three head signals are used for home signals. These protect interlockings, junctions, and crossings, and thus must display an absolute "stop." Intermediate automatic block signals will feature a number plate that results in a red aspect interpreted as a "stop and proceed" (at restricted speed). C&O adopted speed signaling, a system where signal indication governs the speed of a train through interlocking limits.

A General Electric B36-7 still painted for Seaboard System leads a unit coal train on the former C&O at Columbus, Ohio, in August 1988. Today, modern alternating current six-motor diesels are standard power on unit coal trains. It was C&O practice to use cantilever signal bridges, as pictured here. *Bradley McClelland*

Speeds are for a normal, medium, or slow route. The speed of the route is mandated by the track speed through the interlocking. Speed signaling does govern operating speed over the line.

By 1954, most busy C&O mainlines were equipped with three- and four-aspect automatic block signals. Three-aspect gives two-block protection, and four-aspect gives three-block protection. Four-aspect signaling can be used to increase line capacity by reducing the separation between trains. C&O used alternating current to power its signals, with a direct current battery backup. In most installations, a standard, low-voltage direct current track circuit was employed for automatic block. On double- and multiple-track lines with automatic block signals, trains would operate on signal indication in the current of traffic. C&O preferred the use of signal bridges at many installations and typically constructed large cantilever bridges to support signal hardware. The advantage of a signal bridge is that signal heads can be centered over the track they govern.

Today, the C&O color-light arrangement has become standard for new CSX signal installations. Most home signals feature three heads, which have the capability to display normal, limited or medium, and slow speed routes. The aspects follow a C&O system. Although the arrangement of lights generally follows the C&O pattern, the actual hardware employed is of a modern variety. Often, signals are placed on line-side masts instead of on overhead bridges. This is less of a problem in

As late as the mid-1990s much of the former B&O retained traditional signal towers, and many still used mechanical levers and rods to move switch points. The old B&O UN Tower, pictured in July 1988, was located near the east end of the yard at New Castle, Pennsylvania, and was typical of the traditional towers found all along the B&O. In the CSX era, many traditional towers have been closed and demolished. UN Tower was closed as part of a resignaling project in November 1995. *Brian Solomon*

modern railroading than it would have been when C&O installed its color lights in the steam era. Improved forward visibility, made possible with modern supercab diesels, makes sighting signals at speed much easier than it would have been staring down the length of a boiler on a 2-6-6-6 Alleghany. Smoke is less of a problem, too!

RF&P Cab Signals

Richmond, Fredericksburg & Potomac maintained a four-aspect cab signal system in addition to its three- and four-aspect lineside signaling system on the length of its largely double-track mainline. This used a through-the-rail code carrier frequency of 60Hz. With the inclusion of RF&P into the CSX system, this represented an operational anomaly and limited the operation of lead locomotives over the line to those equipped with RF&P cab signal equipment—largely GP40-2s and some former Seaboard System General Electric B36-7s. Until the June 1999 inclusion of Conrail lines, RF&P was the only CSX route with cab signals. In February 1999, in preparation for the operation of Conrail lines, CSX converted the old RF&P system to a 100Hz code carrier system compatible with former Conrail routes. Since many Conrail road locomotives were equipped with a 100Hz system, this allowed significantly greater locomotive fleet flexibility over the old RF&P.

BIBLIOGRAPHY

Armstrong, John H. *The Railroad—What it Is, What it Does.* Omaha, NE: 1982.

Barsness, Richard W. "Hays T. Watkins, Jr." *In Railroads in the Age of Regulation, 1900–1980,* edited by Keith L. Bryant Jr. New York: 1988.

Bell, J. Snowdon. *The Early Motive Power of the Baltimore and Ohio Railroad.* New York: 1912.

Brignano, Mary, and Hax McCullough. *The Search for Safety.* Pittsburgh: 1981.

Bruce, Alfred W. *The Steam Locomotive in America.* New York: 1952.

Bryant, Jr., Keith L. *Railroads in the Age of Regulation, 1900–1980.* New York: 1988.

Castner, Charles B., with Ronald Flanary, and Patrick Dorin. *Louisville & Nashville Railroad—the Old Reliable.* Salem, VA: 1996.

Chernow, Ron. *The House of Morgan.* New York: 1990.

Churella, Albert J. *From Steam to Diesel.* Princeton, NJ: 1998

Daughen, Joseph R., and Peter Binzen. *The Wreck of the Penn Central.* Boston: 1971.

Dixon, Jr., Thomas W. *Chesapeake & Ohio—Superpower to Diesels.* Newton, NJ: 1984.

Dolzall, Gary W., and Stephen F. Dolzall. *Monon—The Hoosier Line.* Glendale, CA: 1987.

Drury, George H. *Guide to North American Steam Locomotives.* Waukesha, WI: 1993.

——. *The Historical Guide to North American Railroads.* Waukesha, WI: 1985.

Farrington, Jr., S. Kip. *Railroading from the Head End.* New York: 1943.

——. *Railroading from the Rear End.* New York: 1946.

——. *Railroading the Modern Way.* New York: 1951.

——. *Railroads at War.* New York: 1944.

——. *Railroads of the Hour.* New York: 1958.

——. *Railroads of Today.* New York: 1949.

Frey, Robert L. *Railroads in the Nineteenth Century.* New York: 1988.

Grant, H. Roger. *Erie Lackawanna—Death of an American Railroad, 1938–1992.* Stanford, CA: 1994.

Harlow, Alvin F. *Steelways of New England.* New York: 1946.

History of General Railway Signal Company. Rochester, NY: 1979.

Holbrook, Stewart H. *The Story of American Railroads.* New York: 1947.

Hungerford, Edward. *Daniel Willard Rides the Line.* New York: 1938.

Ivey, Paul Wesley. *The Pere Marquette Railroad Company.* Los Angeles: 1970.

Jones, Robert W. *Boston & Albany: The New York Central in New England, Vols. 1 & 2.* Los Angeles: 1997.

King, Steve, *Clinchfield Country.* Silver Spring, MD: 1988.

Kirkland, John F. *Dawn of the Diesel Age.* Pasadena, CA: 1994.

Klein, Maury. *History of the Louisville & Nashville Railroad.* New York: 1972.

Marre, Louis A. *Diesel Locomotives: The First 50 Years.* Waukesha, WI: 1995.

Marre, Louis A., and Jerry A. Pinkepank. *The Contemporary Diesel Spotter's Guide.* Milwaukee, WI: 1985.

Marre, Louis A., and Paul K. Withers. *The Contemporary Diesel Spotter's Guide, Year 2000 Edition.* Halifax, PA: 2000.

McDonald, Charles W. *Diesel Locomotive Rosters.* Milwaukee, WI: 1982

Middleton, William D. *Landmarks on the Iron Road.* Bloomington, IN: 1999.

Pinkepank, Jerry A. *The Diesel Spotter's Guide.* Milwaukee, WI: 1967.

——. *The Second Diesel Spotter's Guide.* Milwaukee, WI: 1973.

Potter, Janet Greenstein. *Great American Railroad Stations.* New York: 1996.

Protheroe, Ernest. *The Railways of the World.* London: 1910.

Salisbury, Stephen. *No Way to Run a Railroad.* New York: 1982.

Saunders, Jr., Richard. *Merging Lines: American Railroads 1900–1970.* DeKalb, IL: 2001.

——. *The Railroad Mergers and the Coming of Conrail.* Westport, CT: 1978.

Snell, J. B. *Early Railways.* London: 1972.

Solomon, Brian. *The American Diesel Locomotive.* Osceola, WI: 2000.

——. *The American Steam Locomotive.* Osceola, WI: 1998.

——. *GE Locomotives.* St. Paul, MN: 2003.

——.*Locomotive.* Osceola, WI: 2001.
——.*Railroad Signaling.* St. Paul, MN: 2003.
——.*Railroad Stations.* New York: 1998.
Solomon, Brian, and Mike Schafer. *New York Central Railroad.* Osceola, WI: 1999.
Starr, John W. *One Hundred Years of American Railroading.* Millersburg, PA: 1927.
Staufer, Alvin F. *C&O Power.* Carrollton, OH: 1965.
Stover, John F. *History of the Baltimore & Ohio Railroad.* West Lafayette, IN: 1987.
Thompson, Slason. *Short History of American Railways.* Chicago: 1925.
Vance, Jr., James E. *The North American Railroad.* Baltimore: 1995.
White, Jr., John H. *Early American Locomotives.* Toronto: 1979.
Wilner, Frank N. *The Amtrak Story.* Omaha, NE: 1994.

Periodicals

The Bull Sheet. Baltimore, MD.
CTC Board—Railroads Illustrated. Ferndale, WA.
Diesel Era. Halifax, PA.
Diesel Railway Traction, supplement to *Railway Gazette.* UK.
Extra 2200 South. Cincinnati, OH.
The Home Signal. Champaign, IL.
Jane's World Railways. London.
Locomotive & Railway Preservation. Waukesha, WI.
Official Guide to the Railways. New York.
RailNews. Waukesha, WI.
Railroad History, formerly *Railway and Locomotive Historical Society Bulletin.* Boston, MA.
Railway Age. Chicago and New York.
Railway Gazette, 1870–1908. New York.
The Railway Gazette. London.
Railway Signaling and Communications, formerly *The Railway Signal Engineer* nee, *Railway Signaling.* Chicago and New York.
Richmond Times-Dispatch. Richmond, VA.
Traffic World. Washington, D.C.
Trains, Waukesha, WI.
Vintage Rails. Waukesha, WI.
Washington Post. Washington, D.C.

Brochures, Catalogs, Manuals, Pamphlets, Rule Books, and Timetables

Association of American Railroads. *American Railway Signaling Principles and Practices.* New York: 1937.
CSX Transportation. *Baltimore Division, Timetable No. 2.* 1987.
CSX Transportation. *System Map.* 1999.
CSX Transportation. *Signal Aspect and Indication Rules.* 2001.
General Electric. *Dash 8 Locomotive Line.*
General Electric. *GE Locomotives.*
NORAC Operating Rules, 7th Edition. 2000.
Proceedings of the Institution of Mechanical Engineers. *Diesel Locomotives for the Future.* New York: 1987.
Richmond Fredericksburg and Potomac Railroad Company. *Timetable No. 31.* 1962.

INDEX